♊ Alfred's

Pock[et]
Dictionary
of Music
Terms Composers Theory

Compiled and Edited
by Sandy Feldstein

TABLE OF CONTENTS

PRONUNCIATION GUIDE

ah	broad *a* as in *father*.
ah	the same sound, only not dwelt upon; like *ah* in '*rah!*
ă	short English *a*, as in *mat*.
â	like *a* in *mare*.
ä	like *â*, but closer. Short *ä* is nearly like *e* in *met*, but more open.
ā	like *a* in *mate*.
e, ĕh	short sound of long a.
ĕ	short *e*, as in *met*.
ē	long *e*, like *ee* in *meet*.
ī	long *i*, as in *site*.
ĭ	short *i*, as in *sit*.
ōh	like *o* in *rode*.
o, ŏh	short o, like the first o in *opinion*.
ô	pronounced like *aw* in *saw*.
ö	not found in English. To pronounce long ö, set the lips as if to say "*oh*," and then say "*ā*" (as in *mate*); for short ö set the lips and say "*ĕ*" (as in *met*).
ōō	like long *oo* in *loot*.
ŏŏ	like short *oo* in *look*.
ŭ	short *u*, as in *but*.
ŭh	like the *u* in *fur*.
ü	not found in English. To pronounce long *ü*, set the lips as if to say "*oo*" (as in *loot*), and then say "*ee*" (as in *meet*); for short *ü*, set the lips and say "*i*" (as in *sit*).

Abbreviations Used In This Dictionary

Eng. English
Fr. French
Ger. German
Gr. Greek
It. Italian
L. Latin
Sp. Spanish

Throughout this dictionary, terms within definitions that may be unfamiliar but are defined separately, appear in italic type.

Terms

A

A cappella *(It., ăh cahp pĕl´lăh).*   Choral music without *accompaniment.*

A2.   See *a deux.*

A due *(It., ăh dōō´ĕh).*   See *a deux.*

A deux *(Fr., ăh dö).*   Both players play. Usually used in instrumental music when two parts are notated on one staff, indicating that both play in unison.

A tempo *(It., ăh tĕm´pŏh).*   Return to the original speed or tempo.

Absolute music.   Music composed with no extra musical implications, as opposed to *Program Music.*

Absolute pitch.   The ability of a person to identify a musical sound by name without any previous pitch being sounded. Also called *perfect pitch.*

Accelerando *(It., ăht chĕn lĕh răhn´dŏh).*   Abbr. *accel.* Becoming faster.

Accent.   Indicated with the symbol >. To place emphasis on a specific note.

Acciaccatura *(It., ăht chăh kăh tōō´răh).*   Used in keyboard music of the 17th century. Indicates the playing of a *neighboring tone* and main note simultaneously. The neighbor is released quickly.

Accidentals.   Symbols used to indicate *chromatic* changes, either raising or lowering notes. Sharp (♯), flat (♭), or natural (♮).

Accompaniment. Background for a melody. Could be as simple as a singer accompanied by chords with a guitar, or the left hand of the piano, or as complete as full orchestra.

Accordion. A portable keyboard instrument which produces sound by filling bellows with air that is pushed against reeds, causing them to vibrate.

Acoustic *(āh kōō′ stĭk).* Nonamplified as opposed to electronically amplified. "Acoustic" guitar as opposed to "electric" guitar.

Acoustics. The science of sound.

Ad libitum *(L., ăhd lĭbĭ′ tŭm).* Indicates freedom to interpret within the basic musical context. At the performer's will.

Adagio *(It., āh dāh′ jōh).* Slow between *largo* and *andante* (see tempo chart on page 220).

Added sixth. Adding the sixth note above the root to a *triad*. Most often used in popular music. Ex.: C, E, G, A.

Aeolian *(ā ō′ lē ăn).* The church mode made up of the whole and half step relationship found by playing the white keys of the piano from A to A. (Same as the natural minor. See scale.)

Affabile *(It., ăhf fah′ bĭ lĕh).* Gentle.

Agitato *(It., ăh jē̆ tah′ tōh).* Harried, excited.

Air. Song, usually used referring to music of the 17th and 18th centuries.

Air de cour *(Fr.).* A short *strophic* song.

Alberti bass. Named after Domenico Alberti (d. 1740). Indicates broken chord style, keyboard accompaniment for the left hand.

Aleatory music, Aleatoric music. Chance music where performer and/or composer chooses the elements by a random or chance pattern.

Al fine *(It., ăhl fē´ně).* To the end.

Alla breve *(It., brä´věh).* A *tempo* indication meaning cut time (¢), with the half note rather than the quarter receiving the beat. $\frac{2}{2}$ rather than $\frac{4}{4}$.

Allargando *(It., ăhl lähr gähn´dŏh).* Slowing down.

Allegretto *(It., ăhl lĕh grĕt´tŏh).* Fast, a little slower than *allegro.* Often implies lightness (see tempo chart on page 220).

Allegro *(It., ăhl lä´grŏh).* Tempo marking indicating fast, quick (see tempo chart on page 220).

Allemande *(Fr., ăh lĭ mahńd).* A dance form in a moderate *duple* time. In the late 18th century the German version changed to $\frac{3}{4}$ time.

Alliteration. A group of words that begin with the same letter.

Al segno *(It., ăhl sĕn´yŏh).* Return to the sign.

Alteration. Raising (♯) or lowering (♭) a note.

Altered chord. A chord with *chromatic* changes to one or more notes.

Alto *(It., ahl´tóh)*. A female voice (see chart of voice ranges page 240).

Alto clef. Usually used for viola parts, establishes middle C on the 3rd line of the staff.

C

Amplifier. A device used to increase the power or voltage of any signal.

Amplitude. The difference between the high and low points of a sound wave or sound cycle.

Anacrusis *(L., an uh kroo´sis)*. Upbeat or *pickup*.

Analysis. The theoretical study of the organization of music.

Andante *(It., ähn dähn´téh)*. Tempo marking indicating moderate or walking speed (see tempo chart on page 220).

Andantino *(It., ähn dähn té´nóh)*. A little slower than *andante* (see tempo chart on page 220).

Animato *(It., äh né mah´tóh)*. With spirit, animated.

Antecedent. The first phrase of a musical *period*.

Anthem. A Protestant *choral* work using a religious text.

Anticipation. A *nonharmonic tone* in the melody sounded before the chord in which it is contained.

Antiphonal. Used related to singing or instrumental playing indicating that two or more groups alternate in performing sections or verses of a composition.

Appoggiatura *(It., ăhp pŏhd jăh tōō´ răh).* An ornamental note, usually the lowered second, which is followed by the main note.

Arco *(It., ar´ kŏh).* To bow. Used for string instruments as distinct from *pizzicato*, which means to pluck.

Aria *(It., ah´rē äh).* A song for solo voice with instrumental accompaniment. Usually associated with opera.

Arioso *(It., ah rē oh´zŏh).* Lyrically, expressively.

Arpeggio *(It., ar ped´jŏh).* Notes of a chord which are played one after another.

Arrangement. The setting of a work for a medium other than which it was originally composed.

Ars antiqua *(L., ahrz ăn tē´ kwuh).* Literally meaning the old art, used to indicate the 13th century school.

Ars nova *(L., ahrz nŏ´vuh).* Literally meaning the new art, used to indicate the music of the 14th century.

Art song. A serious composition for voice, usually with accompaniment.

Articulation. The way in which notes are begun and how they are performed. *Staccato* (short) and *legato* (smooth) are articulation instructions.

ASCAP. American Society of Composers, Authors, and Publishers, a performing rights organization that collects royalties for its members.

Attacca *(It., ah tahk´ kah).* Go on. See *segue.*

Attack. The way a sound is initiated.

Atonality. Music without a tonal center.

Audition. When one performs before a reviewer or group of reviewers, usually to determine the performer's ability.

Augmentation. Elongating the duration of a note.

Augmented. Raised, usually related to augmented interval in which the interval is expanded by ½ step. To form an augmented triad the fifth of a major triad is raised ½ step. Ex.: C, E, G♯. See *added sixth.*

Augmented sixth. See *sixth chord.*

Authentic cadence. A cadence that ends with the V chord moving to the I chord.

Auxiliary tone. Also called *neighboring tone*, a tone a step (whole or half) above or below the main tone.

B

Back beat.   A rhythmic style in pop music which emphasizes the 2nd and 4th beats of each measure.

Backup group.   Most commonly the singers behind a lead vocalist.

Bagatelle *(Fr.)*.   A short composition most often written for piano.

Balalaika.   A fretted instrument of Russian origin similar to a guitar. It has 3 strings that are tuned in *fourths*.

Balance.   The adjustment of parts within a group of performers so all can be heard.

Ballad.   A song that tells a story. In pop music it is usually slow in *tempo* and romantic in lyric content.

Ballade *(Fr., bähl lahd́)*.   Although it connotated specific musical elements in various periods of history, today it is used interchangeably with ballad.

Ballet *(băl lāý)*.   A dance form that combines dance with music (and usually costumes and scenery) to depict a story.

Ballo *(It., bähĺ loh)*.   Dance.

Band.   Any group of woodwind, brass, and percussion instruments such as symphonic band, concert band, jazz band. Also used for groups of limited instrumentation such as brass band.

Banjo.   A string instrument used in folk and popular music.

Bar. A term meaning *measure*.

Bar line. Vertical lines that divide music into measures.

Barcarole *(Ger., băhr kăh rŏhl´lĕ).* The names of the boat songs sung by the gondoliers in Venice. May be used to describe other music composed in a similar style.

Baritone. The male voice range between the tenor and bass (see chart of voice ranges page 240).

Baroque. The historic period in music approximately between 1600 and 1750. The music of the Baroque tended to be highly ornamented and sometimes elaborate. Music was mainly written for the church or for the courts of the monarchs.

Bass. The lowest part. Also refers to the lowest of the male voice ranges (see chart of voice ranges page 240).

Bass clef. Also called the F clef, establishes the note F on the fourth line of the staff.

 F

Basso *(It., băhs´sŏh).* Low. Most often used in the abbreviation "8va basso" which means to play one octave below the written note.

Basso continuo *(It., kŏhn tē´nŏŏ ŏh).* See *figured bass*.

Basso ostinato *(It., ŏh stē nah´tŏh).* A repetitive melodic and/or rhythmic figure in the bass part.

Batterie *(Fr.)*.   The percussion section.

Battuta *(It., băht tŏŏ´ tāh)*.   The beat. Often meaning the lst beat or strong beat in a measure. Also used as *a battuta* meaning the same as *a tempo*

Beam.   The horizontal line that connects notes into easily visible groups.

Beam ➝

Beat.   The pulse within music. Four beats to each *measure* means four pulses or counts.

Beats.   An audible, regularly occurring stress within a sustained sound. This occurs when two of the same tones are played together but are not producing the exact same frequencies of sound waves. Thus they are not perfectly in tune.

Bebop.   A style in jazz which began in the 1940s, characterized by small groups, extended harmonies, intricate rhythms, and emphasis on improvisation. Also called bop and rebop.

Bel canto *(It., bĕl kăhn´ tōh)*.   The vocal style that emphasized excellence of sound and performance. Literally meaning beautiful singing or well sung.

Berceuse *(Fr., bâr söz)*.   Lullaby or cradle song.

Bewegt *(Ger., bĕ vāyht´)*.   Animated.

Binary.   A form in music consisting of two parts: A B.

Bitonality.   Two tonalities or key centers employed simultaneously in a musical composition. A common technique used in the 20th century.

Blue notes.   The lowered 3rd, 7th, and sometimes 5th; characteristic of the blues sound. Example in the key of C:

Blues.   Originally work songs and field hollers (country blues), which developed into a 12-*bar* form based on a strict chordal progression. The lowered 3rd and 7th degrees of the scale, called blue notes, are usually evident in the melodic structure.

BMI.   Broadcast Music, Inc., a performing rights organization that collects royalties for its members.

Board fade.   A recording procedure which diminishes the sound on a tape, usually done at the end of a record.

Bolero *(Sp., bōh lēh' rōh).*   A Spanish dance, usually in $\frac{3}{4}$ time.

Boogie-woogie.   A jazz piano style in which the left hand plays a repetitive rhythmic figure.

Bouche *(Fr., boosh).*   Closed. Often used in referring to muted (stopped) horn or, in vocal music, closed mouth — humming.

Bourdon *(Fr., boor dōhń).*   A sustained low note similar to a *pedal point*.

Bourrée *(Fr., bōō ra)*. A bright 17th-century dance usually in duple meter beginning with a *pickup note*.

Bow. A wooden stick with horsehairs attached. The hairs are drawn across the strings of a string instrument to produce its characteristic sound.

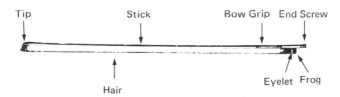

Bowing. The technique of drawing the bow hairs across the strings.

Brace. The term for the bracket that connects staves.

Brass instruments. The family of *wind instruments* which includes: trumpet, cornet, flugelhorn, French horn, trombone, baritone, euphonium, and tuba.

Bravura *(It., brah vōō′räh)*. Spirit, skill. Often used when refering to a composition that requires a high degree of technical proficiency on the part of the performer.

Breit *(Ger., brīt)*. Broad, *largo*.

Bridge. The support over which the strings of stringed instruments are stretched. In composition, it is the short section that connects two main sections. In pop music, it is the middle section or B part (*see ternary form*) of the song.

Bridge passage. The musical material that connects two themes. Often this section is the transition from one *key* to another.

Brio, con (*It., kŏhn brē´ŏh*). With spirit.

Broken chord. Chordal notes played in succession rather than sounded together. See *arpeggio*.

Buffo (*It., bōōf´foh*). Comic, as in opera buffo — comic opera.

Burgundian School. A main center of musical activity during the *Medieval Period.*

Burlesque. A stage show, comic in character, consisting of various, short, unrelated segments.

Byzantine Chant. Musically similar to *Gregorian Chant* but often with nonscriptural texts. Predominant in the Christian church in the Byzantine Empire (300 - 1453).

C

C. The sign for common time ($\frac{4}{4}$).

Caccia *(It., caht´chäh).* Literally, hunt or chase. Usually refers to a strict two-part *canon*.

Cacophony. Dissonance, harshness.

Cadence. A resting point at the end of a phrase, section or complete composition. Also see *perfect cadence*, *authentic cadence*, and *plagal cadence*.

Cadenza *(It., käh děn´zäh).* A solo section that gives the performer a chance to "show off" his or her virtuosity. Some composers write cadenzas in their works, while others indicate that the performer may improvise his or her own.

Calando *(It., käh lähn´dôh).* Gradually diminishing.

Calmando, calmato *(It., kähl mähn´dôh, kähl mah´toh).* Quieting.

Calore *(It., käl lôh´reh).* Warmth.

Cambiata *(It., kähm byäh´tah).* The name given to the adolescent male voice or "changing voice." In counterpoint, it refers to a resolution involving 2 or more tones moving from dissonance to consonance.

Camera *(It., kah´měh räh).* Chamber—referred to music to be performed da camera, in the chamber, outside of the church as opposed to da *chiesa*, to be performed in the church.

Camerata *(It., kăh mĕh răh´ta)*. A name for small schools in the 16th century. A group of people who would get together to discuss the future of their art.

Canon. A form of counterpoint in which one voice begins, followed by another performing the same melody. Similar to a *round*.

Cantabile *(It., kăhn tah´bē lĕh)*. Singing style.

Cantare *(It., kăhn tah´rĕh)*. To sing.

Cantata *(It., kăhn tăh´tah)*. A vocal work for chorus, soloist, and orchestra that is performed without staging.

Canto *(It., kăhn´tŏh)*. Song.

Cantor. A solo singer who sings the solo portions of the religious service. Also used as a title for a church's director of music.

Cantus firmus *(L.)*. The main melody which is used as the theme of a polyphonic composition.

Canzona, canzone *(It., kăhn zoh´năh, kăhn zoh´nĕh)*. A lyrical song.

Cappella *(It., kah pĕl´la)*. A chapel or place of worship in the Middle Ages. Later it meant singers or choir.

Capriccio *(It., kăh prĕt´chŏh)*. A humorous composition.

Capriccioso *(It., kăh prit chŏh´sŏh)*. To be played in a humorous style.

Capstan. The portion of a tape recorder that pulls the tape past the head assembly.

Carillon *(Fr., käh rē yôhń).* A set of bells, originally hung in a church, which are activated by a keyboard.

Carol. Song of praise, usually related to Christmas time.

Castrato *(It., käh strah´ tōh).* The term for men who were castrated as boys so their voices would not change as their bodies grew. Thus when mature, they had the pure vocal sound and range of a soprano or alto, and the chest and lungs of a man. The practice stopped in the 18th century.

Cedez *(Fr., sā´ dä).* To slow down.

Cello *(It., chel´lōh).* See *violoncello*.

Chaconne *(Fr., shäh kōhń).* A variation form based on a repetitive *basso ostinato*. Usually has a continuous harmonic progression above the bass.

Chalumeau *(Fr., shäl lü mōh´).* The lowest register of the clarinet, rich and warm in sound.

Chamber music. Music for a small group of instrumentalists where each part is played by one performer.

Chance music. See *aleatory music*.

Changes. A pop expression meaning the *chord progressions* within a song.

Chanson *(Fr., shähn sōhń).* Song.

Chant. *Monophonic* music which is free in rhythm.

Character piece. 19th-century compositions that conveyed a mood or told a story. Usually for piano and/or solo instrument.

Chart. In jazz and pop music, the written arrangement. If the arrangement is not written, it is called a "head chart."

Chest voice. The low register of one's voice.

Chiesa *(It., kee ĕh′sah).* Church — referred to music to be performed da chiesa, in the church, as opposed to da *camera*, in the chamber.

Choir. A large group of singers often associated with a church. See *chorus.*

Choral. When pronounced with the accent on the first syllable, it refers to a vocal composition. When pronounced with the accent on the second syllable, it refers to a group of singers. Today, the preferred spelling for the latter is *chorale.*

Chorale *(Ger., kōh rahl).* A group of singers. Until the 19th century, it also referred to a hymn tune.

Chorale prelude. An organ composition based on a hymn tune.

Chord. Three or more tones sounded simultaneously.

Chorister. A choir singer.

Chorus. A large group of singers. Often used for school groups and others not associated with a church. See *choir.*

Chromatic. Moving in half steps.

Chromatic scale. A scale that uses all 12 tones within an octave.

Chromaticism. A style of music that includes tones outside the *diatonic* scale.

Church modes. A system of scales most often used in the church music of the Middle Ages. They are all based on the notes of the C Major scale but start on D *(Dorian)*, E *(Phrygian)*, F *(Lydian)*, G *(Mixolydian)*, A *(Aeolian)*, B *(Locrian)*, and C *(Ionian)*. These scales have also been popular in the 20th century.

Circle of fifths. The clockwise arrangement of successive keys arranged in an order of ascending fifths. C, G, D, A, E, B(Cb), F♯(Gb), C♯(Db), Ab, Eb, Bb, F

Clarinet. A single-reed instrument of the woodwind family.

Classical. The musical period from 1750-1820 characterized by the music of Mozart, Haydn, and early Beethoven. The term is often used to differentiate "serious" or "art" music from popular music.

Clavichord. A keyboard instrument of the 15th-18th centuries. Differs from a *harpsichord* in that the string is struck rather than plucked.

Clavier *(Ger., klä vēr).* Keyboard — used to designate the instruments and the music for them (harpsichord, clavichord, and organ) in the Baroque period. From the 19th century on, it designated music for the piano.

Clef. A symbol at the beginning of the staff that indicates what notes are on what lines and spaces. See *treble clef, bass clef, alto clef.*

Close harmony. When a melody is harmonized using the closest chord tones — keeping the melody and bass within an octave.

Clusters. Groups of notes separated by the interval of a *second*. Creates a dissonant sound.

Coda *(It., kōh´däh).* An ending or concluding section.

Codetta *(It., kōh dĕt´täh).* A short *coda*.

Col arco *(It., kōhl ar´kōh).* Related to string instruments — play with the bow.

Col legno *(It., kōhl län´yōh).* Related to string instruments — play with the bow stick, not with the bow hair.

Coll, colla *(It., kōhl, kōhl´äh).* With the.

Coll ottava *(It., kōhl ōht-tah´väh).* With the octave — most often used in keyboard music, means to play the notes and also play them an octave higher.

Coloratura *(It., kōh lōh räh too´räh).* Fast, virtuoso vocal melody.

Combo. Small group of musicians, usually fewer than six.

Comic opera. An *opera*, which has a joyful ending and contains humorous elements.

Common chord. A chord present in two different keys which is used as a bridging element when *modulating* from one key to another.

Common time. $\mathbb{C}$ $\frac{4}{4}$ *meter.*

Common tone. A tone found in two successive chords. When moving from one chord to the other, the tone remains constant.

Composer. One who writes music.

Compound meters. Simple meters multiplied by three. Compound duple ($\frac{6}{2}$, $\frac{6}{4}$, $\frac{6}{8}$), triple ($\frac{9}{4}$, $\frac{9}{8}$), quadruple ($\frac{12}{4}$, $\frac{12}{8}$, $\frac{12}{16}$).

Con *(It., kōhn)*. With.

Concert. A public performance.

Concert pitch. The basic pitch sounded by non-*transposing instruments*, such as the keyboard.

Concertino. The solo group in the Baroque *concerto grosso*.

Concert master. The principal first violinist of an orchestra.

Concerto *(It., kōhn chär´ tōh)*. A composition for soloist and orchestra.

Concerto grosso *(It., kōhn chär´tōh grôs´sōh)*. A baroque concerto which uses two instrumental groups. A small solo group called the *concertino* and the full orchestra called the *ripieno*. The switching from solo group to full orchestra creates interest, variety of sound, and *dynamic* change.

Concord. See *consonance*.

Conducting. The direction of a group of musicians.

Conjunct. Notes that are next to each other in a scale.

Conservatory. A school for musicians.

Consonance. A pleasing combination of sounds.

Con sordino *(It., sohr dē´nôh)*. With *mute*.

Consort. A 16th-century term for chamber group. Also used today with the same basic meaning.

Contralto. See *alto*.

Contrapuntal. In the style of *counterpoint*.

Contrary motion. Two melodies or musical lines going in opposite directions.

Corda *(It., kŏr'dăh)*. String.

Corde *(Fr., kŏr' dĕh)*. String.

Counterpoint. Specifically meaning note against note, it refers to the style of music where two or more melodies are played simultaneously. Their interweaving creates a contrapuntal texture.

Courante (Fr., kŏō răhnt). A 16th-century dance, usually in triple meter, that was one movement of the *suite*.

Crab motion, crab canon. Playing a melody backwards. Starting with the last note and ending with the first.

Crescendo *(It., krĕh shĕn' dŏh)*. Gradually getting louder. Indicated in music by the symbol ◁

Cross rhythm. The simultaneous use of different rhythm patterns that creates a unique texture. Ex.: 3 notes being played against 4 notes with the same time span.

Cue. (1) Small notes in a part that tell one performer what another is playing. Used at the end of a long rest to give an indication of where one is in the music. (2) A conductor's gesture, preparing a performer's entrance.

Cycle. A complete vibration — acousticians talk of music tones in cycles per second.

Cyclic. Musical form including various movements or sections which employ recurring thematic material.

D

Da capo *(It., dah kah´pōh).* From the beginning. Indicates to go back to the beginning.

Damper. A part of the piano *key* mechanism. When the key is depressed, the damper releases the string allowing it to vibrate.

Dal segno *(It., dähl sän´yŏh).* From the sign. Indicates to repeat from the sign. See *segno.*

D.C. Abbr. for *da capo.*

Decay. The dying away of a musical sound.

Deceptive cadence. A cadence that sounds as if it will be final and then does not reach a definite resolution. This is usually accomplished by substituting a VI chord in place of the I chord.

Decibel. The unit for measuring the loudness of sound.

Decrescendo *(It., dā crĕh shĕn´dōh).* Gradually decreasing loudness, indicated by the symbol ⟍⟍⟍⟍⟍⟍. Also *diminuendo.*

Demos. Recordings made to demonstrate a song, a singer, or both.

Descant. An *obbligato* part, or second melody, that is above the main melody.

Descriptive music. See *program music.*

Detache *(Fr., dā tāh shā̃).* Detached style of violin bowing. *Staccato.*

Development. The section of a musical composition where the composer elaborates upon the basic thematic material of the work. See *sonata form.*

Diatonic. Within the whole and half tone system of major and minor scales.

Diminished. Made smaller.

Diminished 7th chord. A chord made up of all minor 3rds. Ex.: E^{o7} = E, G, B♭, D♭.

Diminished triad. A chord made up of two minor 3rds. Ex.: C^{o}: C, E♭ ,G♭.

Diminuendo *(It., dē mē nōō ĕn′dŏh).* Gradually getting softer. Abbr. *dim.*

Diminution. In counterpoint: to diminish or lessen the rhythmic value of notes. Ex.: half notes becomes quarter notes.

Dirge. A composition designed to be performed at a funeral.

Discord. A combination of sounds that is harsh, not pleasing.

Dissonance. Notes that, when sounded simultaneously, cause tension. See *discord.*

Div. Abbr. for *divisi.*

Divisi *(It., dē vē′zē).* Indicates that a large group is divided into two smaller groups. Ex.: 1st violins divisi means that the 1st violin section divides in two groups and plays two different parts.

Divertimento *(It., dē vâr tē mĕn´tŏh).* A light instrumental work of ; multiple short movements.

Dixieland. New Orleans style of jazz which began in the early 1900s. The basic group consists of a trumpet or cornet, clarinet, trombone, piano and/or banjo, bass or tuba, and drums. The style is characterized by contrapuntal improvisation.

Dodecaphonic. *Twelve-tone composition, serial music.*

Dolce *(It., dōhl´chĕh).* Sweetly.

Doloroso *(It., dŏh lŏh rōh´sŏh).* Sorrowful.

Dominant. The 5th degree of the scale.

Dorian. The church mode made up of the whole and half step relationship found by playing the white keys of the piano from D to D.

Dot. A dot after a note prolongs its duration by half the value of its original length. A dot under or over a note denotes *staccato*.

$$\text{♩} \cdot = \text{♩} + \text{♪} \qquad\qquad \overset{\text{♩}}{\cdot}$$

Double bar. Two vertical lines drawn through the staff at the end of a section or composition.

Double concerto. A concerto for two solo instruments and orchestra.

Double counterpoint. See *invertible counterpoint.*

Double flat (♭♭). Indicates to lower a pitch two half steps.

Double reed. Two *reeds* separated by a slight opening. When blown, they vibrate against each other.

Double sharp (×). Indicates to raise a pitch two half steps.

Double stop. Two tones played simultaneously by one player. Most often used in string music.

Downbeat. Beat one of a measure.

Down bow. A sign (⊓) that indicates the bow is be drawn in a downward motion.

Doxology. Hymn song. Today, in the Protestant church, it refers to the verse "Praise God from whom all blessings flow."

D.S. Abbr. for *dal segno.* 𝄋

Due *(It., dōo′ ĕh).* Two.

Duet. A composition for two performers.

Dump. 16th-century English instrumental music.

Duo *(Fr., Ger., Sp.).* Duet.

Duple meter. Grouping of time in units of two. ($\frac{2}{2}$, $\frac{2}{4}$, $\frac{2}{8}$)

Dur *(Ger., dōor).* Major.

Duration. The length of sound.

Dynamic marks.   Indications of various degrees of volume.

  pp = *pianissimo*, very soft
  p = *piano*, soft
  mp = *mezzo piano*, moderately soft
  mf = *mezzo forte*, moderately loud
  f = *forte*, loud
  ff = *fortissimo*, very loud.

Dynamics.   Related to the various degrees of volume.

E

Échappée *(Fr., ā chăp pā)*   Escape tone, a nonharmonic tone approached by step and left by a leap in the opposite direction. Usually occurs on a weak beat.

Écossaise *(Fr., ā kŏh säz)*.   An English country dance of the late 1700s and early 1800s.

Eighth note.   See *notes*.

Eighth rest.   See *rests*.

Einsatz *Ger., īn′ sähtz)*.   Attack or entrance.

Electronic instruments.   Musical instruments that produce their sound totally through electronic means, i.e., synthesizer, organ; or by altering a nonelectronic sound, i.e., electric guitar, electric bass.

Electronic music.   Music produced by electronics. The sounds can be generated electronically or by conventional instruments or a combination of both.

Elegy. A composition depicting a sad feeling, often composed in honor of someone's death.

Eleventh. The distance from the 1st to the 11th notes of a scale.

Embellishment. Added tones that ornament a melody.

Embouchure *(Fr., ähm bōō shür).* The position of the mouth and lips when playing wind instruments.

Ému *(Fr.).* With feeling, emotion.

Encore *(Fr., ähn kŏr).* An extra piece, usually short in duration, performed at the end of a concert when the audience's applause indicates great enthusiasm.

Enharmonic. Two tones that sound the same but are spelled differently are enharmonic. C♯ is the enharmonic equivalent of D♭.

Ensemble *(Fr., ähn sähm bl).* A group of musicians (instrumentalists or singers) who perform together. The term ensemble is often used to describe the precision with which a group plays together.

Entr'acte *(Fr., ähn trähkt).* A composition (usually instumental) performed between the acts of a play, opera, or musical comedy.

Envelope. Primarily used when discussing electronic music. Envelope refers to the attack and decay of a sound.

Episode *(ĕp´ ĭs sōd)*.   A second section not including the main theme. Usually used related to *Fugue:* a section that does not contain the subject.

Equal temperament.   See *temperament*.

Equalizer.   A device that increases or decreases the strength of a sound signal in selected portions of the audible spectrum, usually used in the mastering process of recording.

Escape note.   See *échappée*.

Espressivo *(It., eh sprĕs se´vŏh)*.   Expressively.

Ethnomusicology.   The study of music within a cultural context.

Ethos *(Gr., ē´thōs)*.   The character of different scales conceived by the ancient Greeks. They believed different scales implied different feelings such as strong, passionate, etc.

Étouffé *(Fr.)*.   Damped, muted.

Etude *(Fr., ā tüd´)*.   A composition or study designed to teach specific techniques on an instrument or a group of instruments.

Etwas *(Gr., ĕt´vähss)*.   Somewhat.

Eurhythmics.   A system of teaching rhythm through movement developed by Emile Jacques Dalcroze.

Evaded cadence.   A cadence that is prepared for a particular resolution, and then resolves in a different manner.

Exposition. The section of a composition that first exposes the thematic material. See *sonata form*.

Expression marks. Signs or words which indicate how the performer should interpret the notes and rhythm. i.e., *tempo, dynamics, articulation*, etc.

Expressionism. Developed as a reaction to Impressionism in the visual arts. In music it tended to be abstract with limited emotional involvement.

Extemporization. See *improvisation*.

F

F. Abbr. for *forte*.

F-hole. See *sound hole*.

Fagott (*Ger., fäh gōhí*). Bassoon.

Fake book. A book that contains the basic melodies, chords, and lyrics of many popular songs.

False cadence. See *deceptive cadence*.

Falsetto. The light, high register of the male voice. It is above the normal range, and is less powerful than the normal voice.

Fandango. A Spanish dance, usually in triple meter with emphasis on the second beat.

Fanfare. In today's usage, an opening, usually brilliant and ceremonial. Often played by brass instruments.

Fantasia *(It., fähn täh zē´äh).* A composition in free form.

Fantasy. See *fantasia.*

Farandole *(Fr., fäh rähn döhl´).* A dance (usually in $\frac{6}{8}$), one of the most famous is from L'Arlésienne, by Bizet.

Feedback. An imbalance of input and output in a sound system which causes a yowling noise in the speakers.

Feminine cadence. When the final chord occurs on a weak beat.

Fermata *(It., fär mah´täh).* To hold or pause. In music, indicated by the sign ⌒, meaning to hold longer than the normal duration of the note.

FF. Abbr. for *fortissimo.*

Fiddle. Slang name for violin.

Fifth. The distance from the 1st to the 5th notes of a scale.

Figure. See *motif, motive.*

Figured bass. Most popular in the *Baroque* era, a bass part was indicated with numbers (figures beneath). They indicated the harmonies to be sounded above the bass note.

Finale *(It., fē nah´lĕh).* The last section or movement of a work.

Fine *(It., fē´nĕh).* The end.

Fingerboard. The section of stringed instruments where the fingers press on the strings to produce different pitches.

First-movement form. See *sonata form.*

Five, The Russian. A group of 19th-century composers who wrote in a very nationalistic style (Cui, Borodin, Balakirev, Mussorgsky, and Rimsky-Korsakov).

Flamenco. A Spanish song performed with guitar accompaniment and often danced.

Flat (♭). The musical symbol that indicates to lower the pitch of a note by one half-step.

Flemish school. 15th- and 16th-century composers from the Netherlands and Belgium who had a major influence on the development of the *polyphonic* style.

Flourish. (1) A trumpet *fanfare*. (2) A passage with a lot of *ornamenation*.

Folk music, folksong. Music that is transmitted orally from generation to generation, usually unique to a specific locale.

Form. The design of a musical composition.

Forte *(It., fôhr´těh)*. Loud. Abbr. *f*

Fortissimo *(It., fôhr tis´sẽ mõh)*. Very loud. Abbr. *ff*

Forzando, forzato *(It., fôhr tsähn´ dŏh, fôhr tsäh´tŏh)*. Forced, accented.

Fourth. The distance between the 1st and 4th notes of a scale.

Fourth chord. Any chord made up of intervals of a fourth.

French overture. See *overture*.

French sixth. See *sixth chord*.

Frequency. The number of cycles of sound waves produced each second. Frequency determines pitch.

Fret. A thin strip of metal placed across the fingerboard of guitars and other string instruments.

Frog. The end of the bow of a stringed instrument that is held in the player's hand.

Fugato *(It., foo gah´tōh).* In the style of a fugue. Usually a section of a non-fugal composition, often in the developmental section.

Fughetta *(It., few geh´ta).* A short *fugue*.

Fugue *(fewg).* A contrapuntal style in which each voice enters at a different time playing the same melody. Similar in concept to a round or canon, but usually more complex musically.

Fundamental. The lowest note of a harmonic series.

Fuoco, con *(It., kōhn fwōh´kōh).* With fire.

G

Galliard *(Fr., gähl yard´).* A 16th-century dance characterized by compound duple meter and *hemiola*.

Gavotte *(Fr., gäh vōht´).* A 17th-century dance in moderate time, usually starting with an upbeat of two quarter notes.

Gebrauchsmusik *(Ger., gĕ brōuchs´ mōō zik).* Functional music, music used in everyday life. The term was coined by the 20th-century composer Hindemith.

General pause. See *grand pause*.

German sixth. See *sixth chord*.

Gesang *(Ger., gĕ zăhnǵ).* Song.

Gesangvoll *(Ger., gĕ zăhnǵ fōhl).* Songlike.

Gestopft *(Ger., gĕ shtŭ́ pft).* Stopped. A technique of inserting the hand in the bell of a French horn to produce a specific tone color.

Gig. A job, slang in the pop genre.

Gigue *(Fr., zhēg).* A standard dance movement in suites from 1650-1750. The most popular type is characterized by compound duple time and dotted rhythms.

Giocoso *(It., jóh kōh́ zŏh).* Humorous.

Glissando *(It., glĭs sǎhń dŏh).* A continuous sliding of pitch from one note to another, notated by a straight or wavy line.

G.P. Abbr. for *grand pause* or *general pause.*

Grace note. A short note preceding a main note.

Grace Note ♪♩ Main Note

Grandioso *(It., grähn dē ōh́ zŏh).* Grand or noble.

Grand pause. A break or extended *rest* in the music. Abbr. *G.P.*

Grand staff. See *great staff.*

Grave *(It., grah' vĕh).* Grave, solemn.

Great staff. The combination of bass and treble staves.

Gregorian chant. The liturgical chant of the Roman Catholic Church named after Pope Gregory I.

Grosse caisse *(Fr., grōs kăss).* Bass drum.

Ground bass. See *basso ostinato.*

Gruppetto, gruppo, groppo. *(It., grŏop pĕt' tōh, grŏop' pōh, grô' pōh).* Italian names for *ornaments.*

Gusto, con *(It., gŏo' stŏh).* With zest.

H

Habanera *(Sp., hăh băh nă' răh).* A Cuban dance in moderate meter.

Half note. See *notes.*

Half rest. See *rests.*

Half step. The distance between two adjacent notes on the piano keyboard.

Harmonic. See *harmonics, overtone series.*

Harmonic analysis. The study of chords and/or harmonies within a composition.

Harmonic minor. The form of the minor scale that is made up of w½ww½ 1½ ½ (w = whole step ⌴ , ½ = half step ∨ , 1½ = 1½ steps ⌣).

Harmonics. High tones, very clear and pure in sound.

Harmony. The result produced when pitches are sounded simultaneously, such as chords.

Harpsichord. A keyboard instrument similar to the piano. The difference being that the strings are plucked by a quill rather than struck by a hammer.

Hasting *(Ger., hāhs´tïg)*. Hurry.

Head voice. The high register of a voice.

Heldentenor *(Ger.).* A very strong tenor voice usually associated with the "hero" roles in Wagner operas.

Hemiola, hemiolia. The change of rhythmic feeling within a composition. The relationship usually is 3 to 2.

Hertz. The name for "cycles per second," named after the German scientist Heinrich Hertz. Abbr. *Hz.*

Heterophony. An improvisational type of performance when two slightly changed versions of the same melody are performed simultaneously. This is an important element of many primitive folk musics.

Hidden fifths, octaves. See *parallel fifths, octaves*

Hold. See *fermata*.

Homophony. One voice supported by a chordal accompaniment.

Hook. The catchy part of a song's story that is most likely to intrigue the audience.

Humoresque. A name for light, humorous instrumental compositions.

Hymn. A song of praise to God.

Hyper-, hypo-. Higher and lower related to the Greek modes. Hyper starts a 5th above the initial tone and hypo starts a 5th below.

I

Ictus *(L.)*. Related to performance of Gregorian chant; a stress or accent.

Idiomatic style. A passage or composition written with the complete understanding of a specific instrument.

Imitation. The same theme or motive repeated in a different part or line. Usually used in a contrapuntal composition, the imitation usually begins on a different pitch.

Impressionism. A term mainly related to the music of Debussy and Ravel. As in painting, it was less formal and evoked a feeling or impression of something. Most prominent in the late 1800s and early 1900s.

Impromptu *(Fr.).* Used as a title for short pieces suggesting an extemporized style.

Improvisation, extemporization. Creating music spontaneously. Although done by musicians in all periods, it is most closely associated with jazz and rock performances.

Incidental music. Short pieces that connect acts of plays.

Incomplete cadence. When the soprano note of the *tonic* chord is not the key-tone.

Instruments. The name for all mechanisms that produce musical sounds.

Interlude. A short piece that is played between sections of a composition or a dramatic work.

Intermezzo *(It., ĭn tĕr mĕd´zŏh).* Similar to incidental music played between the acts of a serious play or opera.

Interval. The distance between two pitches.

Intonation. Exactness of pitch production.

Intrada *(It., ĭn trăh´dăh).* An opening piece or introduction.

Introduction. A preparatory section of a composition.

Introit *(L., ĭn trō´it).* The initial chant of the Mass.

Invention. Originally a title used for Bach's keyboard pieces, today used for pieces in a contrapuntal style.

Inversion. (1) Harmonic: The transfering of a lower pitch of an interval an octave higher, or a higher pitch an octave lower. (2) Melodic: The changing of each ascending interval into the corresponding descending interval.

Inverted mordent. An 18th-century ornament wherein the written note is alternated with the note immediately above it as a short rapid trill.

Invertible counterpoint. Music composed so that the lowest part can also be played above the upper part. If applied to two parts, the method is called *double counterpoint*.

Ionian. The church mode made up of the whole and half step relationship found by playing the white keys of the piano from C to C (same as the *major mode*).

J

Jam. In jazz and rock, collective improvisation based on a familiar tune or chord progression.

Janizary music. Music of the Turkish military bands.

Jazz. Afro-American music, always containing an element of improvisation. Its historical development since the 1900s includes the diverse styles of: Dixieland (or New Orleans style), Chicago style, third-stream, swing, bebop, progression jazz, jazz-rock, and fusion.

Jig. A popular 16th-century English dance.

Jota *(Sp., hōh′ tāh).* A dance from northern Spain in fast $\frac{3}{4}$ time.

Jubiloso *(It., yōo bē lōh′zōh).* Jubilant.

Just intonation. A system of tuning in which all intervals are derived from the natural fifth and third.

K

Kanon. German for canon.

Key. (1) Tonal center or main pitch to which all others in a composition are related. (2) The part of the action of an instrument that is depressed by the player's fingers.

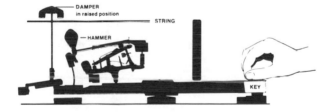

Keyboard. The set of keys on pianos, organs, harpsichords, or other similar instruments. The modern piano keyboard contains 88 keys, thus the slang expression "playing the 88."

Keynote. The note that is the tonal center of a key. See *key* and *tonic*.

Key relationship. The relationship between two different keys.

Key signature. Indicates the sharps or flats in any key. Appears at the beginning of each staff.

Kit. A slang term for drum-set.

Klavier *(Ger., kläh vēr′)*. See *clavier*.

Klingen. To sound.

Koechel listing. The chronological identification of Mozart's compositions organized by L. Von Koechel.

Kyrie *(Gr., kü′rē ēh)*. The first section of the Ordinary of the Roman Catholic Mass.

L

Lacrimoso *(It., läh crē mōh′zōh)*. Mournful, tearful.

Laisser. Usually used as *laissier vibre*, to let vibrate.

Laisser vibre. See *laisser*.

Lament. A composition that is composed in honor of someones death. Sometimes used for any composition designed for use on mournful occasions.

Lamentoso *(It., lä mĕn tōh′sŏh)*. Mournfully.

Lancio, con. With vigor.

Langsam *(Ger., lähng′zähm)*. Slowly.

Largamente *(It., lăr găh měn′ těh)*.   Broadly.

Largando *(It., lăr găhn′ dŏh)*.   Gradually broadening.

Larghetto *(It., lăr gĕt′ tŏh)*.   Somewhat faster than *largo* (see tempo chart on page 220).

Largo *(It., lăr′gōh)*.   Very slow (see tempo chart on page 220).

Larynx.   The organ at the top of the windpipe that produces vocal sounds.

Leader.   Used to refer to a conductor or concert master — one who leads the other musicians.

Leading tone.   The 7th step of the scale a half step below the tonic

Leap.   A skip from one note to another.

Lebendig *(Ger., lĕh bĕn′ dĭyh)*.   Lively.

Lebhaft *(Ger., lāb′ häft)*.   Lively.

Ledger lines.   Also written *leger*.   Short lines used to indicate pitches above or below the staff.

Ledger Lines

Legando *(It., lĕh găhn′ dŏh)*.   Smoothly. See *legato*.

Legato *(It., lĕ gah′ tŏh)*.   Indicates that a passage is to be played very smoothly without interruption between notes.

Leger lines. See *ledger lines*.

Leggero, leggiero *(It., lĕd jä´rōh)*. Light, swift.

Legno *(It., län´yŏh)*. Wood. See *col legno*.

Leicht *(Ger., lï̄yht)*. Light, brisk.

Leiser *(Ger., lï̄´zer)*. Softer.

Leitmotiv, leitmotif *(Ger., lï̄´mōh tēf́)*. Thematic idea or motif associated with a particular character, situation, or idea most often associated with the composer Richard Wagner.

Leno *(It., lä´nòh)*. Quiet, gentle.

Lento *(It., lĕn´tŏh)*. Slow (see tempo chart on page 220).

Lesto *(It., lä´stŏh)*. Gay, lively.

Letter notation. The use of letters to identify tones. Used today for beginning instructive purposes.

L.H. Abbr. for left hand.

Liberamente*(It., lē bĕh räh mĕń tĕh)*. Freely, with liberty.

Libretto *(It., lē brĕt́tŏh)*. The text of an opera, oratorio, or other musical work. In popular music the text is called lyrics.

Lieblich *(Ger., lēṕ lïyh)*. Lovely, sweet.

Lied *(Ger., lēd).* Song. Usually applied to 19th-century German art songs.

Lieto *(It., lie'tō).* Joyful.

Ligature. (1) A 13th- to 16th-century sign that combines two or more notes. (2) In the clarinet family, the adjustable band that holds the reed on the mouthpiece.

Liscio *(It., le'shoh).* Smooth.

L'istesso tempo *(It., lē stěs'sōh).* The same tempo.

Liturgical drama. 12th- and 13th-century medieval plays which represent Biblical stories.

Liturgy. The service of a Christian church, particularly Roman Catholic.

Loco *(It., lō'kōh).* Place. Return to the normal octave. Used after 8va. Also see *octave*.

Loudness. The intensity of sound. Similar to volume.

Lourde *(Fr., loord).* Heavy.

Louré *(Fr., loorā).* A type of bowing where the notes within a slur are slightly separated.

Luftig *(Ger., lōof'tiyh).* Light.

Luftpause *(Ger., lōof pǎu'sä).* A short pause.

Lungo, lunga *(It., lōōn′gō, lōōn′gah).* Long.

Lustig *(Ger., lōōs′tĭg).* Cheerful.

L.V. Abbr. for *laisser vibre.*

Lydian. The church mode made up of the whole and half step relationship found by playing the white keys of the piano from F to F.

Lyre. Ancient Greek string instrument held and strummed by hand or with a pick.

Lyric. (1) The text of a popular song. (2) In a smooth, melodic style.

M

Ma *(It., măh).* But. Ma non troppo, but not too much.

Madrigal. A name for Italian vocal music of the 14th and 16th centuries. The madrigal style was also used in England in the late 1500s and early 1600s.

Maestoso *(It., măh ě stōh′sōh).* Majestic.

Maestro *(It., măh ěh′ströh).* Teacher. Usually used referring to conductor.

Maggiore *(It., mah jō′rěh).* Major mode.

Main *(Fr., măn).* Hand. main droit — right hand, main gauche — left hand.

Majeur *(Fr.).* Major mode.

Major, minor. Used to describe *scales, chords, intervals, keys.*

Mancando *(It., măhn kähn dōh).* Dying away.

Mano *(It., mah nōh).* Hand. Mano destra — right hand, mano sinistra — left hand.

Marcato *(It., mar kăh tŏh).* Marked, accented.

March. Music designed to promote uniform group marching.

Marcia *(It., mar chăh).* March.

Mariachi *(Sp.).* A group of Mexican folk musicians.

Marque *(Fr.).* Stressed.

Martele *(Fr.)* Hammered. A style of bowing in which all strokes are hammered.

Marziale *(It , mar tzē ah lēh).* Martial.

Masculine cadence. When the final chord occurs on a strong beat.

Masque, mask. A 16th- and 17th-century stage production usually based on a mythological subject.

Mass. The Roman Catholic church service.

Mässig *(Ger., mä sĭg).* Moderately.

Mazurka *(măh zōōr kăh).* A Polish folk dance in triple meter employing extensive use of dotted rhythms.

Measure. The distance between two bar lines.

Medesimo *(It., měh dā´zē mŏh).* The same.

Mediant. The 3rd degree of the scale.

Medieval period. The historic period in the arts, approximately between 600 and 1450.

Medley. In pop music, an arrangement that links together two or more songs.

Mélange *(Fr., mā lahń zh).* A medley.

Melisma. In vocal music, many notes sung to one syllable.

Melody. Single pitches sounded one after another.

Meno *(It., mā´nŏh).* Less. Meno *mosso,* less motion.

Mensural notation. A system of notation used until 1600 that indicated the duration of each note.

Menuet *(Fr.);* **Menuett** *(Ger.).* See *minuet.*

Messa di voce *(It., měs´sāh dē vōh´chěh).* A vocal technique of the 18th century. A note is begun softly and gradually gets louder and then returns to its starting volume.

Meter. The pattern of fixed beats by which a piece of music is measured. Meter is indicated by a *time signature.*

Metronome. A clock-type mechanism that clicks beats. It is adjustable to any tempo, slow through fast.

Mezzo, mezza *(It., měd´zŏh, měd´zăh).* Half, moderately.

Microtone. An interval smaller than a half step. Part of the music of many non-Western cultures; also found in contemporary Western music since the 1900s.

Middle Ages. The period from 600 to 1450.

Middle C. The C in between the treble and bass staff. It is near the middle of the piano keyboard.

Miniature score. The score of a musical composition reproduced in a small size for study purposes.

Minor. See *major.*

Minuet. A French country dance in $\frac{3}{4}$ meter, usually performed in a moderate tempo.

Mirror canon. A canon which sounds the same when performed backwards as when performed forwards.

Missa *(L.).* Mass.

Misterioso *(It., mē stěh rē ŏh´sŏh).* Mysteriously.

Mit *(Ger., mĭt)*.   With.

Mixer.   A device that makes a composite signal out of two or more input signals.

Mixing.   A recording procedure in which the output from the several channels on a strip of tape, each containing different voices and/or instruments, is electronically blended into one (monaural) or two (stereo).

Mixolydian.   The church mode made up of the whole and half step relationship found by playing the white keys of the piano from G to G.

Modal.   Pertaining to the modes.

Modality.   Music based on the modes.

Mode.   Notes arranged in a scale, that form the basic tonal material of a composition.

Moderato *(It., mŏh dĕh rah´ tŏh)*.   Moderate speed (see tempo chart page 220).

Modern.   The period in music from 1900 to today characterized by continual change. Highly influenced by technology.

Modulate.   To change from one key to another.

Modulation.   To change from one *key* to another within a composition.

Moll *(Ger., mōhl)*.   C *moll*, C minor.

Molto *(It., môhl´ tōh)*.   Very — Molto *allegro*, very quick.

Monophony, monophonic.   Music with a single melodic line without accompaniment. See *texture*.

Monothematic.   A piece based on one theme.

Monotone.   Originally related to reciting a liturgical text on one pitch. In slang, refers to one who cannot vocally match a pitch.

Mordent *(Ger., môr´ dĕnt)*.   A musical ornament or embellishment consisting of the alternation of the written note with the one immediately above or below it.

Morendo *(It., môh rĕn´ dōh)*.   Dying away.

Mosso *(It., môhs´ sōh)*.   Agitated, moved.

Motet.   A polyphonic form of the Middle Ages and Renaissance periods. Later used to describe various choral compositions.

Motif, motive.   A melodic and/or rhythmic idea that is used as a unifying element in a composition.

Moto *(It., mô´ tōh)*.   Motion — *con* moto, with motion.

Mouthpiece.   The part of the *wind instruments* which is placed on or between the players lips.

Movement. A complete and somewhat independent section of a larger work.

Multitracking. Recording procedure where each voice or instrument is recorded on a separate portion of the tape and then mixed together. See *mixing* and *overdub*.

Music drama. The original description of *opera*.

Musicology. The scholarly study of music.

Musique concrete *(Fr., mü zēk kŏhn krĕt).* Concrete music — music composed from recorded sounds which are electronically modified.

Mute. A device put on or in a musical instrument to muffle or soften its tone.

N

Nach *(Ger., näh).* After.

Nachtmusic *(Ger., näht moo zĭk).* Night music, a serenade.

Nach und nach *(Ger., näh oont näh).* Little by little.

Naked fifth. *Open fifth.*

Nationalism. A style of music that is based on nationalistic elements.

Natural (♮). The musical symbol that indicates a note is neither *sharp* nor *flat*.

Neapolitan school.   An 18th-century school of composition centered around Naples.

Neapolitan sixth.   The first inversion of a chord built on the lowered second degree of the scale. In the key of C: F A♭ D♭ .

Neck.   The part of string instruments on which the *fingerboard* lies.

Neighboring tone.   A nonharmonic note a step above or below another note.

Neoclassicism.   A school of 20th-century composition that reacted against the overly romantic style by returning to forms and ideas prevalent in the classical period.

Neumes.   The symbols used to indicate notation in the *Middle Ages*.

Ninth.   The interval of an *octave* plus a *second*.

Nocturne *(Fr., nŏhk´ tŭrn)*.   A romantic composition, usually for piano.

Node.   The place on a vibrating object which remains at rest.

Nonet.   A piece for nine performers. Also can refer to a group of nine performers.

Nonharmonic tones.   Notes that embellish a melody and are not part of the basic harmony.

Notation.   The way one writes music. The system shows pitch and rhythm in a way that musical ideas can be performed by anyone know-ing the notational system.

Notes. The symbols used to write music.

o	whole note
♩	half note
♪	quarter note
♪	eighth note
♪	sixteenth note
♪	thirty-second note

Nuance *(Fr., nü ahnss´).* A subtle shading in *dynamics, tempo,* or *phrasing.*

Nut. A part of string instruments at the upper end of the *neck* which is used to raise the strings over the *fingerboard.*

O

Obbligato *(It., ŏhb blē gah´ tŏh).* Originally meant that a part should not be omitted. Today it means an additional part similar to a *descant.*

Oblique motion. When one part moves while the other remains stationary.

Oboe family. A group of double reed instruments which include the oboe, English horn, bassoon and contra bassoon.

Octave. The distance from one pitch to the same letter name; 12 half steps (8 notes) apart. Abbr. *8va* indicates to play one octave higher; *8va basso* indicates to play one octave lower.

Octet. A piece for eight performers. Also can refer to a group of eight performers.

Ode. A musical work of praise.

Offertory (*L., offertorium*). The 4th part of the Roman Catholic Mass.

One-half step. The distance from one key on the piano to the next black or white adjacent key.

Open fifth, open triad. The sounding of a 5th without including the 3rd.

Open harmony. When the chord tones are spread over more than an *octave*.

Opera. A sung drama, accompanied by an orchestra, presented on stage with sets.

Opera bouffe (*Fr., òh' pā ràh boōf'*) **opera buffa** (*It., òh' pā ràh boōf' fàh*). See *comic opera*.

Opera comique (*Fr., òh' pā ràh kòh mēk'*). See *comic opera*.

Opera seria (*It., òh' pā ràh sā'rē àh*). Serious opera.

Operetta *(It., ŏh´ pĕh rĕt´ tāh)*. A short opera, usually light in content or in a popular style.

Opus *(L.)* Literally work, a number used to designate the chronological position of a work within a composer's output.

Oratorio *(It., ŏh rāh tó´ rē ŏh)*. A composition for voices and instruments with a sacred or Biblical text.

Orchestra. A large ensemble of instruments. Today's orchestra consists of four main sections: *strings*, *woodwinds*, *brass*, and *percussion*.

Orchestration. The designation of which instruments play which parts of a composition.

Ordinary and proper. In the Roman Catholic *liturgy*, the ordinary portion of the service remains the same thoughout the year. The proper is variable.

Organ. A keyboard instrument that produces sound by forcing wind through pipes of various lengths. Today this is often done electronically.

Organum *(L., ôr gàn´ ŭm)*. Early polyphonic music from the 9th through the 13th century.

Ornamentation. The embellishing of musical lines. Ornamentation may be improvised by the performer, indicated with a graphic sign, or written in standard notation.

Ornaments. The notes which embellish musical lines. See *ornamentation*.

Oscillator. A device that produces alternating current in the form of sine waves. In electronic music, it has become common practice to call any audio generator an oscillator.

Oscilloscope. An instrument employing a cathode-ray tube which graphically displays the characteristics of an input signal.

Ossia *(It., ŏhs sē´ăh).* An alternate version.

Ostinato *(It., ŏh stē nah´tŏh).* A repeated melodic and/or rhythmic motive.

Ottava *(It., ŏht tah´ vàh).* Octave, abbr. 8va, indicates that the notes should be played one octave higher than written; ottava, 8va bassa, indicates that the notes should be played one octave lower than written.

would be played

would be played

Overblow. To force extra air through a wind instrument. This results in the sounding of harmonics.

Overdubbing. A contemporary recording technique that allows one to record "on top of" previously recorded material.

Overtone series. The frequencies which vibrate above a note (called the fundamental).

The dark notes tend
to be flat in pitch.

Overture. An instrumental piece usually functioning as an introduction to a dramatic work.

P

P. Abbr. for *piano*.

Pantomime. Performance in which the actors do not speak or sing. The plot is told in gestures, movements, and facial expressions.

Parallel chords. The moving of the same chord up or down a scale. It creates a sliding non-tonal center effect and was widely used in Impressionistic music.

Parallel (consecutive) fifths, octaves. The movement of 2 parts in the same direction, a 5th or an octave apart. This was avoided in harmonic practice from the 15th to 19th centuries.

Parallel key. Major and minor keys that have the same key tone.

Parallel motion. Movement of 2 parts when the interval separating them remains the same.

Parlando, parlante *(It., păr lähń dōh, păr lähń tĕh)*. Spoken style, clear and crisp.

Partita *(It., păr tē´tăh)*. Variation. Used in a title to indicate the form of a composition. Usually implied a *suite* of variations.

Passacaglia *(It., păhs săh cahl´yăh)*, **passacaille** *(Fr., păh săh cah´ē)*. Similar to a *chaconne* but often without the harmonic progression.

Passage.   A section or portion of a composition.

Passepied *(Fr., păhs p'yă)*.   A French dance in $\frac{3}{8}$ or $\frac{6}{8}$ meter, usually with spirit.

Passing tone.   A non-chordal tone that moves between two chord tones in a stepwise motion. This usually occurs on a weak beat. When on a strong beat, it is called an *accented* passing tone.

Passionato, passionata *(It., păhs sē ōh năh' tōh, păhs sē ŏn năh' tă)*.   Passionate.

Passion music.   A musical setting of the text of the Passion.

Pastorale *(It., păhs tōh rah' lĕh)*.   A composition with an open natural feeling. Originally written in imitation of the music of shepherds, often using flutes.

Patch cord.   A wire with two plugs, one on each end, used to connect the output of one device to the input of another.

Pathétique.   With great emotion.

Patter song.   In the musical theater, an up-tempo tune, the text of which is usually light or humorous.

Pause.   Also known as a "hold" or *fermata*. Indicates to hold the note (or rest) longer than indicated.

Pavane, pavenne *(păh vahn')*.   Italian dance of the 16th century. Usually slow and in $\frac{4}{4}$ meter.

Pedal point.   A note, usually in the bass, which is held while the harmonies change in the other voices.

Pedal tone.   A sustained or continually repeated note, usually in the bass.

Pentatonic scale.   A scale with five tones to the octave. Popular in music to teach young children because the lack of semitones makes improvisatory experience most enjoyable.

Ex.: Pentatonic scale built on C

⊔ = whole step
⌄ = 1½ steps

Percussion instruments.   Name for instruments that are sounded by striking one object with another, or by shaking.

Perfect cadence.   The progression from dominant to tonic root position chords with the tonic note in the soprano.

Perfect pitch.   See *absolute pitch.*

Period.   A group of measures that make up a natural division of a melody.

Perpetual canon.   A canon whose final cadence leads back to the opening measure so it can be repeated over and over.

Pesante *(It., pĕh sähn′ tĕh).*   Heavily.

Peu à peu *(Fr., pö äh pö).*   Little by little.

Phrase, phrasing.   A musical line that states an idea or thought.

Phrygian.   The church mode made up of the whole and half step relationship found by playing the white keys of the piano from E to E.

Pianissimo *(It., pē äh nēs' sē möh)*.   Very soft. Abbr. *pp*

Piano *(It., pē ah' nŏh)*.   (1) Soft; abbr. *p* (2) The keyboard instrument.

Piano quartet.   A composition for four performers: piano, violin, viola, and cello.

Piano quintet.   A composition for five performers: piano and *string quartet*.

Piano score.   An arrangement for piano of a work composed for a larger medium, usually orchestra or band.

Piatti *(It., pyaht' tē)*.   Cymbals.

Picardy third.   The raising of a minor 3rd ½ step, resulting in making a composition in a minor key end with a major tonality.

Pickup.   See *upbeat, anacrusis.*

Pitch.   The highness or lowness of a sound.

Pitch names.   The name of the notes. C, D, E, F, G, A, B or Do, Re, Mi, Fa, Sol, La, Ti.

Pitch pipe.   A small instrument used to set the pitch for a choir. It is blown in to produce specific notes.

Più *(It., pyōō)*.   More. Più *allegro*, more quickly.

Pivot chord.   In *modulation*, a chord common to both the old and the new key.

Pizzicato *(It., pit sē kah' tōh)*.   Plucking the string.

Plagal cadence.　Ending with a IV-I harmonic progression.

Plainsong.　A style of *monophonic chant*.

Plectrum.　A pick used to activate the strings on fretted instruments.

Poco a poco *(It., pô´kŏh ah pô´kŏh).*　Little by little.

Polka *(pōl´kăh).*　A dance in quick $\frac{2}{4}$ or $\frac{4}{4}$ meter.

Polonaise *(Fr., pŏh lŏh näż).*　A stately Polish dance in triple meter.

Polyphony, polyphonic.　Music that combines more than one musical line. The interaction of the melodies creates its own harmony.

Polytonality.　Many keys. Relates to 20th-century compositions where more than one key is employed simultaneously.

Pomposo *(It., pŏhm pŏh´sōh).*　Pompously, majestic.

Ponticello *(It., pŏhn tē chĕl´lŏh).*　The bridge of stringed instruments. *Sul* ponticello, at the bridge.

Portamento *(It., pŏr tăh mĕn´tōh).*　Gliding from one note to the next.

Position.　(1) Spacing of notes within chords. (2) On string instruments, the various placements of the hand up and down the fingerboard. (3) On trombone, the points at which the slide is held in order to play different notes.

Postlude.　A composition played at the end of a service, usually for organ.

Poussé, poussez *(Fr., poo sā)*.   Up-bow.

PP.   Abbr. for *pianissimo*. Very soft.

Praeludium *(L., prā loo'dē oom)*.   Prelude.

Prelude.   Music designed to be played as an introduction.

Premiere.   The first performance of a composition.

Prepared piano.   A practice in contemporary music where objects are placed on the piano strings to alter their sound.

Prestissimo *(It., prĕh tēs'sē moh)*.   As fast as possible (see tempo chart page 220).

Presto *(It., prä'stōh)*.   Very fast (see tempo chart on page 220).

Prima donna *(It., prē mäh dŏn'nä)*.   Main singer of the female role of an opera. In slang it is used to imply a conceited operatic star.

Prime.   See *unison*.

Primo, secondo *(It., prē'moh, sĕh kŏhn'dōh)*.   First, second.

Program music.   Music inspired by a nonmusical idea, usually descriptive or pictorial.

Progression.   The movement from one note or chord to another. In pop music, the chord progression is often referred to as "the *changes*."

Progressive jazz.   A jazz style of the 1950s characterized by flowing lines and "cool" rather than harsh sounds. Sometimes call the "West Coast" sound.

Pronto *(It., prŏhn´ tōh).* Swiftly.

Psalm. A sacred poem or song.

Psalter *(sôl´ tŭhr).* The Book of Psalms.

Pulse. A beat.

Q

Quadrille *(Fr., kwō dril).* A 19th-century French dance performed in a square. The music alternates between $\frac{6}{8}$ ($\frac{3}{8}$) and $\frac{2}{4}$ meter.

Quadruple meter. Meters based on a subdivision of four ($\frac{4}{2}$, $\frac{4}{4}$, $\frac{4}{8}$.)

Quadruplet. Four notes that are performed in the time of three of the same kind.

$$\overbrace{| \ | \ | \ |}^{4} \ = \ | \ | \ |$$

Quality of tone. The characteristics of a specific vocal or instrumental tone.

Quartal harmony. Harmony built on the interval of a fourth.

Quarter note. See *notes.*

Quarter rest. See *rests.*

Quarter tone. One half of a half step.

Quartet. A piece for four performers. Also can refer to a group of four performers.

Quasi *(It., kwah´zē).* As if, nearly.

Quick step. A march.

Quintet. A piece for five performers. Also can refer to a group of five performers.

Quintuple meter. 5 beats in a measure.

Quintuplet. Five notes that are performed in the time of four of the same kind.

Quodlibet *(L.).* A composition developed by combining many well known melodies or texts. Like a musical potpourri.

R

Raga. A mode or melodic configuration found in the music of India.

Ragtime. A jazz-influenced style of pop music of the early 1900s. It had a recurrence of popularity in the 1970s after being used as the score for a popular movie, *The Sting*.

Rallentando *(It., rähl lĕn tähn´ dōh).* Abbr. *rall.* Gradually slowing.

Range. Related to voice or instruments, the notes playable or singable from the lowest to the highest.

Recapitulation. The return of the main themes. See *sonata allegro*.

Recital. A performance by one or two performers. Also used for *chamber music* recitals.

Recitative *(It., rĕs´ ĭ ta tĕv´).* A speaking voice style used in opera to tell the plot and bridge the gap between *arias*.

Reed. A thin strip of cane which, when set into vibration, produces a musical sound.

Refrain. In folk and popular music, the chorus that is repeated after each stanza.

Register. (1) Different parts of the range of instruments and/or voice. (2) For organ, the pipes controlled by one *stop*.

Registration. Indication of which stops or registers are to be combined for a specific organ passage.

Relative major. A major key is relative to a minor key whose tonic lies a minor third below its own.

Relative minor. A minor key is relative to a major key whose tonic lies a minor third above its own.

Relative pitch. The ability to sing or name any pitch after being given one for a point of reference.

Religioso *(It., rĕh lē jōh´ sŏh).* In a religious or solemn style.

Renaissance Period. The music of 1450 - 1600, characterized by a strong emphasis on cultural ideals and humanistic values.

Repeat. Signs that indicate to repeat a musical section. ‖: :‖

Reprise *(Fr., rŭ prēź).* Repetition. In classical music it is sometimes used interchangeably with *recapitulation*. In show music, it means the repetition of any strong song from a previous section of the show.

Requiem Mass. Mass for the dead.

Resolution. The progression of chords towards a resting point.

Resonance. When vibrations are transferred from one object to another. Ex.: The string on a violin transfers the vibrations to the wooden body of the instrument.

Rests. Silence, symbols that indicate silence.

- ▬ whole rest
- ▬ half rest
- 𝄽 quarter rest
- 𝄾 eighth rest
- 𝄿 sixteenth rest
- 𝅀 thirty-second rest

Retrograde. Backward. Although used since early times, the compositional technique of developing a theme by beginning with the last note and ending with the first was most prevalent in *twelve-tone* composition.

R.H. Abbr. for *right hand*.

Rhapsody. A composition in a free style.

Rhythm. The organization of beats or pulses in time.

Rhythm and Blues. A form of pop music characterized by simple melodies and harmonies, strong rhythms and elements of the blues.

Rhythm section. In pop music, the piano, bass, drums, and guitar which form the rhythmic and harmonic support for the other instrumentalists.

Ripieno *(It.).* In the *concerto grosso* indicates the orchestra as different from the soloists or *Concertino.*

Ritardando *(It.).* Abbr. *rit., ritard.* Gradually slowing down.

Ritenuto *(It., rē těh nōō′ tōh).* Slowing down immediately.

Ritornello *(It., rē tŏr něl′lōh).* A short section at the end of a work, usually restating something that happened before. Also, a recurring instrumental section that returns between solo sections in Baroque music.

Rock. A generic term for the many styles of pop music that have developed from *Rock 'n' Roll.*

Rock 'n' Roll. A form of pop music originated in the 1950s. It developed as an outgrowth of *Rhythm and Blues.*

Rococo. A mid-eighteenth-century style (1725 - 75) which reacted against the grandeur of the Baroque era.

Roman school. A style of composition centered around Rome in the 1500s.

Romance. Short songs usually lyrical in style. They can be for voice or instruments.

Romantic period. The musical period from 1820 - 1900 characterized by strong individualism and nationalism. Composers tended to allow their emotions to openly be expressed in their music.

Rondeau. In poetry and music, a form that is characterized by many returns of a stanza or theme. This developed into the *rondo* form.

Rondo, rondo form *(rōhn' dōh).* A form characterized by the return of the 1st theme. In its simplest form, it would be the same as ternary form (ABA). Usually it is a five part form (ABACA) but can continue with more returning themes, such as ABACABA, etc.

Root. The fundamental note of a chord from which it gets its name.

Rosin, resin. A substance applied to the hair of a bow to give it more friction on the strings.

Round. A tune that can be played or sung with itself, each entrance starting at a specified time in the melody. Similar to a *canon*.

Row. See *tone row*.

Rubato *(It., rōo bāh' tōh).* Freely. Slightly slowing down or speeding up as one interprets a particular music passage.

S

Salsa. A modern Latin American dance style of pop music often combined with Rock rhythms (salsa rock).

Saltato, saltando *(It., săhl tah' tōh, săhl tahn' dōh).* A style of bowing where the bow bounces off the string. Usually used for staccato playing.

Sanctorale *(L.).* The feasts of the Saints.

Sanctus *(L.)*.   The 4th section of the ordinary of the Mass.

Sanft *(Ger., zähnft)*.   Soft.

Sans *(Fr., sähn)*.   Without.

Santillé *(Fr., sŏh tē yā)*.   A style of bowing. See *saltato*.

Saraband.   A triple meter dance of the 17th and 18th century, usually played slowly with emphasis on the 2nd beat.

Saxophone.   A single reed, conical bore instrument invented in the mid-1800s, most popular in jazz and rock music.

Scale.   The arrangement of notes within a specific tonal setting. The arrangement of whole steps (w) and half steps (½) give the scale its character. The major scale consists of a ww½www½. The pure (natural) minor scale consists of w½ww½ww. The harmonic minor scale consists of w½ww½1½½. The melodic minor consists of w½wwww½ ascending and the natural minor descending. The chromatic scale consists of all ½ steps. The whole tone scale consists of all w steps. The pentatonic scale consists of w1½ww1½.

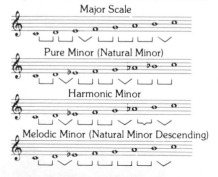

Major Scale

Pure Minor (Natural Minor)

Harmonic Minor

Melodic Minor (Natural Minor Descending)

V – half step
⊔ = whole step
‿ = 1½ steps

Scale degrees. The names and numbers of each note of the scale: (I) tonic, (II) supertonic, (III) mediant, (IV) subdominant, (V) dominant, (VI) submediant or superdominant, and (VII) subtonic or leading tone.

Scat. A type of improvisatory jazz singing which uses syllables rather than words.

Scenario. A sketchy outline of a play or opera.

Scherzando *(It., skâr tsähn′ dōh)*, **scherzhaft** *(Ger., shârts′ häht)*. Playful.

Scherzo *(It., skâr′ tsōh)*. Joke. A $\frac{3}{4}$ composition, bright in tempo. Usually the third movement of a larger work.

Schnell *(Ger., shnĕl)*. Fast.

Schneller (Ger., schnĕl′ ŭh). Another name for an *inverted mordent*.

Schola cantorum *(L., schō′ lä cán′ tŏr′ ŭm)* The singing school organized by St. Gregory. Often refers to any choir which performs Gregorian chants.

Scordatura *(It., skōhr dāh tōō´ rāh).* Tuning a string instrument differently than usual in order to play special passages which contain unusual chords or difficult passages, also used for special effects.

Score. The musical notation that shows all the parts of a composition.

Secco recitative *(It., sĕk´ kōh).* Dry *recitative.* A style of recitative that was not very melodic and lacked expression.

Second. The distance between the 1st and 2nd notes of a scale.

Secondary dominant. A *dominant* chord built on a 5th above any other chord. Usually acts as an *embellishing* chord outside the *key.*

Segno *(It., sān´yŏh).* A sign (𝄋) used to indicate the beginning or end of a section to be repeated.

Segue *(It., sā´gwĕh).* Follows. Proceed to the next section without a break.

Sehr *(Ger., zār).* Very much.

Sel-sync. A device that cancels the time delay between the record and playback heads on a tape recorder.

Semitone. Same as *one-half step.*

Semplice *(It., sĕm´plē chĕh).* Simple.

Sempre *(It., sĕm´prĕh).* Always.

Senza *(It., sĕn´tsāh).* Without.

Septet. A piece for 7 performers. Also can refer to a group of 7 performers.

Sequence. Repetition of a motive or phrase beginning at another pitch.

Serenade. A vocal or instrumental piece, usually light in style.

Serial music. An outgrowth of *twelve-tone* or *dodecaphonic* music in which other aspects of music composition as well as pitch are set up in specific orders. This term is often used interchangeably with the others.

Seventh. The distance between the 1st and 7th notes of a scale.

Seventh chord. A chord made up of a root, 3rd, 5th, and 7th. The most important 7th chord is built on the 5th degree of the scale and is called the dominant seventh or V^7.

Key of C Major V^7

Sextet. A piece for 6 performers. Also can refer to a group of 6 performers.

Sforzando, sforzato *(It., sfŏhr tsahn´ dŏh, sfŏhr tsah´ tŏh).* Abbr. *sf, sfz.* Forced, a sudden stong accent.

Shanty, chanty, chantey. Sailors' work songs.

Shape-note. A system by which different shapes are used to indicate different notes of the scale.

Sharp (♯).   The musical symbol that indicates to raise the pitch of a note one half step.

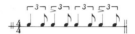

Shift, shifting.   Moving from one position to another on string instruments.

Shofar.   A biblical instrument made from a ram's horn.

Shuffle.   Rhythmic style in which the emphasis is on the 2nd and 4th beats in $\frac{4}{4}$ time. Often with a jazz feeling.

Sideman.   Any musician in a band or orchestra.

Similar motion.   Movement of two parts in the same direction when the interval separating them changes.

Simile *(It., sē´mē lĕh)*.   Continue in a similar style.

Simple meter.   All *duple*, *triple*, or *quadruple* meters. Also see *compound meter.*

Singspiel *(Ger., zĭng´ shpēl)*.   A style of opera that contains spoken diaglogue between musical selections.

Sinistra *(It., sē nĭ´străh)*.   Left.

Sitar.   An Indian lute made popular by Ravi Shankar.

Six-four chord. The 2nd inversion of a triad.

Six,les. *(Fr.).* A group of six 20th-century composers — Louis Durey, Arthur Honegger, Darius Milhaud, Germaine Tailleferre, Georges Auric, and Francis Poulenc.

Sixteenth note. See *notes*.

Sixteenth rest. See *rests*.

Sixth. The distance between the 1st and 6th notes of a scale.

Sixth chord. The first inversion of a triad.

Sixth chords which contain an augmented sixth include the augmented sixth (Italian sixth), the augmented six-five-three (German sixth), the augmented six-four-three (French sixth), and the doubly augmented six four three.

Slide. (1) In string playing, sliding from one note to another. (2) The movable part of the trombone.

Slur. A curved line drawn over two or more notes indicating they are to be played *legato*.

Soave *(It., sŏh ah´vĕh).* Sweet.

Solfège *(Fr., sŏhl fĕdǵ),* **solfeggio** *(It., sŏhl fĕd´jŏh).* The study of reading music by assigning a syllable to each note: Do, Re, Mi, Fa, Sol, La, Ti.

Solo *(It., sŏh´lŏh).* A composition or section for one performer.

Sonata *(It., sŏh nah´täh).* A multimovement composition for solo instrument with or without piano accompaniment.

Sonata allegro. A large *ternary* (ABA) form popular with composers since the 1800s. It consists of *exposition, development,* and *recapitulation* often preceded by an introduction and followed by a coda. See *sonata-form.*

Sonata da camera, sonata da chiesa *(It.).* Chamber sonata, church sonata. See *camera* and *chiesa.*

Sonata form. Also called **sonata-allegro form.** It is divided into 3 main sections. The *exposition* usually consists of 2 themes (the 1st in the tonic key and the 2nd in the dominant). The *development* uses material from both themes and many keys, and the *recapitulation* which repeats the exposition, but this time with both themes in the tonic key. An introduction and coda are also often present.

Sonatina *(It., sŏh nah tē´nah).* A short sonata.

Song. A vocal composition with text or lyrics.

Song cycle. A large musical work made up of many related songs.

Song form. Another name for *ternary form* (ABA).

Sonaro, sonara *(It., sŏh nŏ´rŏh, sŏh nŏ´räh).* Sonorous.

Sopra *(It., sŏh´prah).* Above.

Soprano *(It., sŏh prah´ nŏh).* The highest ranged female voice. (See chart of voice ranges page 240).

Sordino *(It., sŏhr dē´nŏh).* Mute.

Sostenuto *(It., sŏh stĕh nōō´tŏh).* Sustained.

Sotto voice *(It., sŏht´tŏh vŏh´chĕh).* In a soft voice.

Sound hole. The opening cut in the belly of a stringed instrument.

Sound post. A small piece of wood that transfers the vibrations from the belly to the back of a string instrument.

Soundboard. The resonating surface over which piano and harp strings are stretched.

Spacing. The arrangement of notes of a *chord*.

Species. The five basic *contrapuntal* techniques of instruction.

Spiccato *(It., spĭk kah´tŏh).* A separated, detached style of bowing.

Spirito, spiritoso *(It., spē´rē tŏh, spē rē tŏh´sŏh).* Spirit, spirited.

Spiritual. A traditional black song, sacred in character.

Sprechstimme *(Ger., shprĕch´shtĭm mŭh).* Speech song. A type of singing half speaking.

Staccato *(It., stăhk kah´tōh)*.   Detached, played short. Indicated by a dot over or under the note head.

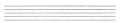

Staff, stave.   The horizontal lines on which notes are written.

Stanza.   One poetic unit of a song.

Step.   A unit for measuring *intervals*.

Stop.   The handle or switch with which an organist regulates which row of pipes will be activated.

Stretto *(It., strĕt´tōh)*.   Repetitive imitation of the subject of a *fugue* characterized by the overlapping of entering voices.

String quartet.   Music for an ensemble of 4 string instruments: 2 violins, viola, and cello.

String instruments.   Instruments which produce sound from a stretched string.

Strophic.   A song in which all stanzas of the lyrics are sung to the same music. Opposite of *through composed*.

Subdominant.   The 4th degree of the scale. Named because it is a 5th below the tonic.

Subito *(It., sōo´bē tōh)*.   Suddenly.

Subject.   The melody or motive that forms the core of a composition.

Submediant. The 6th degree of the scale.

Suite *(süēt).* An instrument form consisting of a number of movements. Traditionally, all movements were dance forms.

Sul *(It.).* On. Sul G = on the G string.

Sul ponticello *(It., pŏhn tē chĕl´lōh).* Play near the bridge.

Sul tasto *(It., tăh´ stōh).* On the fingerboard.

Super tonic. The 2nd degree of the scale.

Sur *(Fr.).* On. Sur G = on the G string.

Suspension. A tone which is sustained while the harmony changes. The suspended tone creates a dissonance with the new harmony.

Swing. Big band jazz of the 1930s.

Symphonic poem. Orchestral music based on an extra musical idea.

Symphony. A composition for orchestra.

Syncopation. Rhythm that is not based on the regular strong and weak beat concept. Although common in all styles, it is most prevalent in jazz.

Synthesizer. An instrument that creates sound electronically.

System. Two or more staves that are connected.

T

Tablature. The name for early systems of notation. Today used as a system for guitar and banjo notation for performers who cannot read standard musical notation.

Tacet. Silence. Usually used to indicate that one should not play an entire section or movement.

Tag. Final ending in a composition. See *coda*.

Tango *(Sp.)*. An Argentinian dance.

Tanto *(It., tähn' tōh)*. So much. Non tanto, not so much.

Tarantella *(It., täh rähn tĕl' läh)*. A $\frac{6}{8}$ Italian dance.

Tardo, tardamente *(It., tär' dōh, tär däh mĕn' tĕh)*. Slow, slowly.

Tardando *(It., tär dähn' dōh)*. Gradually slowing down.

Taste *(Ger., tä' stĕ)*. Key of piano, organ, or other keyboard instrument.

Tasto *(It., tah' stōh)*. (1) Fingerboard of the violin. (2) Key of a keyboard.

Technic. The technical aspects of performing music.

Technique. See *technic*.

Te deum *(L., tä dā' ŭm)*. A song of praise.

Tema *(It., Sp., tá´mäh).* Theme.

Temperament. Any system of tuning where the intervals are different than the acoustically pure one. Equal temperament is the principle of dividing the octave into twelve equal semitones.

Tempo *(It., tĕm´pōh; pl. tempi).* The speed of a composition.

Tempo marks. Terms used to indicate the tempo of a composition.

Tenor. (1) The highest male voice (see chart of voice ranges page 240). (2) In early counterpoint, the part that carried the melody.

Tenuto *(It., tĕh no͞o´tōh).* Indicated by a dash above or below a note, indicates to hold the note for its full value.

Ternary form. Three part form ABA.

Tertian harmony. Common western harmony based on thirds and triads.

Tessitura *(It., tĕs sē to͞o´räh).* The range that is most consistently used within a work or section of a composition.

Tetrachord. Four pitches within the interval of a perfect fourth. Based on the pattern — whole step, whole step, ½ step.

Texture. The basic fabric of a composition made up by the various elements used by the composer.

Theme. A main musical idea of a composition.

Theme and variations. A musical form which states the main idea followed by modifications of it.

Theory, musical. The study of melody, harmony, and other aspects of musical composition.

Third. The distance between the 1st and 3rd notes of a scale.

Third-stream. Music combining jazz with classical music.

Thoroughbass. See *figured bass*.

Through-composed. A song that has new music composed for each stanza. Opposite of *strophic*.

Tie. A curved line joining two notes of the same pitch. They are played as one.

Time. A term used to mean *meter* or *tempo*. In pop music, it is used to indicate even and steady rhythm. Ex.: "The drummer has good time" means that he keeps a steady beat.

Time signature. A symbol indicated at the beginning of a piece of music which shows the unit of beats within a composition.

Toccata *(It., tŏhk kah′ tāh)*. A composition in free style, originally for keyboard instruments.

Tonal.   Music based on tonic-dominant harmony.

Tonal and real.   Related to fugue analysis: it is real if the answer is an exact transposition of the subject, tonal if not exact.

Tonality.   A system of organization in which one pitch becomes the tonal center.

Tone.   The quality of a sound.

Tone cluster.   A group of tones close together which produce a dissonant sound.

Tone color.   The quality of sound produced by one instrument or voice as compared to another playing the same pitch.

Tone poem.   See *symphonic poem*.

Tone row.   The organization of the twelve tones used by composers of twelve-tone (*serial*) music.

Tonguing.   The use of the tongue to articulate on wind instruments.

Tonic.   The main note of a key.

Tono *(It., tô′nōh)*.   Tone.

Tosto *(It., tô′stōh)*.   Quickly.

Touch.   The way the keys are depressed when playing the piano.

Touche *(Fr., tōōsh)*.   (1) Fingerboard of the violin. (2) Key of the piano.

Tr. Abbr. for *trill*.

Transcription. The arrangement of a composition for voices or instruments other than those for which it was originally composed.

Transition. A short section that leads from one main part of a composition to another.

Transposing instruments. Instruments that produce a sound different from their written note.

Transposition. The changing of a composition from one key to another.

Tre *(It., trā).* Three.

Treble clef. Establishes the note G on the second line of the staff.

Tremolando *(It., trēh mōh lăhń dōh).* With tremolo.

Tremolo *(It., trâ´mōh lōh).* The rapid repetition of a single note.

Triad. A three note chord generally consisting of root, 3rd, and 5th.

Trill. The rapid alternation of two adjacent notes.

Trio *(lt., trē´oh).* (1) Music for three players. (2) The middle section in the scherzo or minuet movement.

Triple meter, time. With a pulse built on three's ($\frac{3}{2}$. $\frac{3}{4}$. $\frac{3}{8}$).

Triplet. Three notes that are performed in the time of two of the same kind.

Tritone. The interval of the *augmented* 4th or *diminished* 5th.

Troppo *(lt., tróp´pōh).* Too. *Allegro* non troppo, not too fast.

Troubadour. Traveling poets and musicians prominent in southern France in the 12th and 13th centuries.

Tune. Melody.

Tuning. Adjusting an instrument to its proper pitch.

Tuning fork. A steel fork which produces a pure pitch.

Turn. A group of four or five notes used to embellish a main note.

Tutti *(lt., tōō´tē).* All. Ex.: everyone plays together.

Twelve-tone technique. See *serial music.*

Two-part form. See *binary form.*

U

Un peu *(Fr., ön pö)*. A little.

Un poco *(It., ön pô´kŏh)*. A little.

Una corda *(It., ōu´näh kôr´däh)*. One string. When playing the piano: depressing the left pedal (soft pedal) causes the hammer to strike one or two strings rather than the two or three which are struck in normal playing.

Unequal voices. Mixed voices, men and women.

Unison. (1) Everyone plays or sings the same melody. (2) The interval made when sounding two of the same pitches (Ger., Prime).

Unruhig *(Ger., ōon rōo´ig)*. Restless.

Upbeat. *Anacrusis*, pickup. Notes that occur before the first complete measure.

Up-bow. A sign (∨) that indicates the bow is to be pushed in an upward motion.

Ut supra *(L., ŭt sŭ´prä)*. As before.

V

Valse *(Fr., vähls)*. *Waltz*.

Valve. A device on brass instruments that makes it possible to play all of the chromatic notes.

Valve instruments. Brass instruments with valves.

Vamp. In show and popular music, a short accompaniment type pattern that is repeated at will.

Variation. The changing or developing of a musical idea in a way that one can recognize characteristics of the original.

Vaudeville *(Fr., võh d' vēl).* (1) Popular shows of the early 1900s made up of comedy and songs. (2) In the 1700s, a short song with a text about love.

Venetian school. A name given to a group of Flemish and Italian composers who lived in Venice, Italy.

Veranderungen *(Ger., fĕr an' dă rūn gĕn).* Variations.

Verhallend *(Ger., fŭr hähl' lent).* Fading away.

Verse. In pop music, the changing section of text that tells the story followed by the *refrain*, which is the same each time.

Vibrations. A sound wave moving back and forth from its highest to its lowest point.

Vibraphone. A keyboard percussion instrument with motor-driven butterflies in each resonator which pulsate the air column and cause a *vibrato* type effect.

Vibrato *(It., vē brăh' tŏh).* A rapid fluctuation of pitch slightly above or below the main pitch.

Vigoroso *(It., vē gŏh rōh' sŏh).* With vigor.

Viol. The name given to stringed instruments in the 16th and 17th centuries.

Viola *(It., vē ō´lah).* The second member of the violin family, tuned a fifth lower than the violin.

Violin. The highest pitched and probably the most important string instrument. The most famous violin makers were: Niccolo Amati (1596 - 1684), Antonio Stradivari (1644 - 1737), and Giuseppe B. Guarneri (1698 - 1744).

Violin family. Made up of the string instruments: violin, viola, cello, and double bass.

Violoncello *(It., vē ōh lōhn chěl´lōh).* The tenor voice of the string family.

Virginal. An early type of *harpsichord*.

Virtuoso *(It., vēr tōō oh´sōh).* A musician with the highest degree of technical ability.

Vivace *(It., vē vah´chěh).* Lively, very quick.

Vivo *(It., vē´vōh).* Lively.

Vl. Abbr. for *violin*.

Vla. Abbr. for *viola*.

Vlc. Abbr. for *violoncello*.

Vocalise *(Fr., voh cäh lēz´).* See *vocalization*.

Vocalization. A vocal warm-up exercise where many notes are sung on one vowel.

Voce *(It., vōh´chĕh).* Voice.

Voice. (1) The human instrument for producing sound. (2) Any single melody or line in polyphonic music.

Voice-leading. The smooth movement of parts from one chord to another.

Voices. The human voice is usually named related to its range. From low to high, they are bass, baritone, tenor (male voices); alto (contralto), mezzo soprano, soprano (female voices).

Voicing. (1) The way the notes of a chord are arranged. (2) In piano, the adjustment of the hammers to produce the desired tone quality.

Voile *(Fr.).* Veiled, subdued.

Voix *(Fr., vwăh).* Voice.

Volti *(It., vŏhl´tē).* Turn the page.

Volti subito *(It., vŏhl tē sōō´bē tŏh).* Turn quickly. Abbr. *v.s.*

Volume. The loudness or softness of sound.

Voluntary. Originally a composition played before or after a church service.

Vorspiel *(Ger., fōhr´shpēl).* Prelude.

V.S. Abbr. for *volti subito.*

W

Waldhorn *(Ger., vählt´ horn).* A natural horn with or without valves.

Waltz. A dance in moderate $\frac{3}{4}$ time.

Wehmutig *(Ger., vā mü´ tïyg).* Sad.

Well tempered. In equal *temperament.*

Whistle. A small, end-blown pipe, made of wood, cane, metal, or plastic.

Whole note. See *notes.*

Whole rest. See *rests.*

Whole tone. The interval of a major 2nd, or two half steps.

Whole tone scale. A six note *scale* made up of whole tones.

Wind instruments. Any instrument which generates sound by a vibrating column of air.

Wind machine. A device that imitates the sound of the wind.

Woodwinds. The family of *winds instruments* which includes: flutes. double reeds (oboe, bassoon), clarinets, and saxophones.

Word painting. Illustrating non-musical ideas through musical means.

Wuchtig *(Ger., vōhh tïyg).* Heavy, with weight.

Wurdig *(Ger., vür´ diyg).* With dignity.

X

Xylophone. A keyboard percussion instrument whose bars are made of hard wood.

Y

Yodel. A style of Swiss and Austrian mountain region singing or calling.

Z

Zapateado *(Sp., thāh pāh tā äh´ dō)*. A Spanish solo dance characterized by syncopated heel stamping.

Zeltmass *(Ger., tzīt´ mähs)*. Tempo.

Ziemlich *(Ger., tsēm´ liyh)*. Rather. Ziemlich schnell, rather fast.

Zither *(Ger., tsit´ ter)*. (1) A hand-held string instrument used in the folk music of Bavaria and Austria. (2) Also refers to the many string instruments of similar ilk.

Zusammen *(Ger., tsū sämēn)*. Together, used after *divisi (Ger., geteilt)*.

Zwei *(Ger., tsvī)*. Two.

Zwischenspiel *(Ger., tsvish´ēn shpēl)*. Interlude.

Composers

A

Adler, Samuel

BIRTH: March 4, 1928 — Mannheim, Germany
TEACHER(S): Piston, Thompson, Hindemith, Geiringer
COMPOSITIONAL MEDIA: orchestra, chamber music, keyboard, choral, opera, songs
ITEMS OF INTEREST: teacher — Eastman School, NY

Albéniz, Isaac

BIRTH: May 29, 1860 — Camprodón, Spain
DEATH: May 18, 1909 — Cambo-les-Bains, France
TEACHER(S): Brassin and Gevaert at Brussels Conservatory, Jadassohn and Reinecke at Leipzig Conservatory, Dupont
COMPOSITIONAL MEDIA: orchestra, keyboard, choral, opera
ITEMS OF INTEREST: child prodigy, settled in Paris in 1893, best known works include orchestral piece "Iberia"

Alberti, Domenico

BIRTH: 1710 — Venice, Italy
DEATH: 1740 — Formio or Rome, Italy
TEACHER(S): Lotti
COMPOSITIONAL MEDIA: keyboard, choral, opera
ITEMS OF INTEREST: Alberti bass is named after him

Amram, David Werner

BIRTH: November 17, 1930 — Philadelphia, PA
TEACHER(S): Giannini
COMPOSITIONAL MEDIA: orchestra, chamber music, choral,
opera, songs, theatrical, jazz, film, T.V.
ITEMS OF INTEREST: composer-in-residence — New York Philhar-
monic, 1966-67

Anderson, Leroy

BIRTH: June 29, 1908 — Cambridge, MA
DEATH: May 18, 1975 — Woodbury, CT
COMPOSITIONAL MEDIA: orchestra
ITEMS OF INTEREST: best known works include "The Syncopated
Clock," "Sleigh Ride," "Typewriter," all originally composed for the
Boston Pops Orchestra

Antheil, George

BIRTH: July 8, 1900 — Trenton, NJ
DEATH: February 12, 1959 — New York
TEACHER(S): Bloch, Von Sternberg, Smith
COMPOSITIONAL MEDIA: orchestra, ballet, keyboard, choral,
opera, books
ITEMS OF INTEREST: compositions, such as "Ballet Mecanique,"
incorporate mechanically produced sounds

Arlen, Harold

BIRTH: February 15, 1905 — Buffalo, NY   DEATH: April 23, 1986
TEACHER(S): his father, Simon Bucharoff
COMPOSITIONAL MEDIA: songs, popular, film and/or T.V.
ITEMS OF INTEREST: best known works include the song "Stormy
Weather"

Arnold, Malcolm (Henry)

BIRTH: October 21, 1921 — Northampton, England
TEACHER(S): Jacob
COMPOSITIONAL MEDIA: orchestra, chamber music, opera, ballet, songs, film, T.V.
ITEMS OF INTEREST: professional trumpeter

B

Babbitt, Milton

BIRTH: May 10, 1916 — Philadelphia, PA
TEACHER(S): Bauer, James, Sessions
COMPOSITIONAL MEDIA: orchestra, keyboard, songs, electronic, jazz
ITEMS OF INTEREST: teacher — Princeton University, Director — Columbia-Princeton Electronic Music Center

Bach, Johann Christian

BIRTH: September 5, 1735 — Leipzig, Germany
DEATH: January 1, 1782 — London, England
TEACHER(S): J.S. Bach, Karl Philipp Emanuel Bach, Padre Martini
COMPOSITIONAL MEDIA: orchestra, chamber music, keyboard, choral, opera
ITEMS OF INTEREST: youngest son of J.S. Bach, taught Mozart

Bach, Johann Christoph

BIRTH: December 8, 1642 — Arnstadt, Germany
DEATH: March 31, 1703 — Eisenach, Germany
COMPOSITIONAL MEDIA: organ, choral
ITEMS OF INTEREST: uncle of J.S. Bach

Bach, Johann Christoph Friedrich

BIRTH: June 21, 1732 — Leipzig, Germany
DEATH: January 26, 1795 — Bückeburg, Germany
COMPOSITIONAL MEDIA: orchestra, keyboard, choral, songs
ITEMS OF INTEREST: second-youngest son of J.S. Bach

Bach, Johann Sebastian

BIRTH: March 21, 1685 — Eisenach, Germany
DEATH: July 28, 1750 — Leipzig, Germany
COMPOSITIONAL MEDIA: orchestra, chamber music, keyboard,
choral
ITEMS OF INTEREST: the most important composer of the early
1700's, developed the style of contrapuntal writing to its
zenith — most famous for sacred cantatas, St. Matthew and St. John
Passions, and B-Minor Mass, as well as keyboard works (e.g. Well-
Tempered Clavier and two and three part inventions)

Bach, Karl (often spelled "Carl") Philipp Emanuel

BIRTH: March 8, 1714 — Weimar, Germany
DEATH: December 14, 1788 -- Hamburg, Germany
TEACHER(S): J.S. Bach
COMPOSITIONAL MEDIA: orchestra, chamber music,
keyboard, choral, books
ITEMS OF INTEREST: second surviving son of J.S. Bach,
taught his brother J. Christian Bach

Bach, Wilhelm Friedemann

BIRTH: November 22, 1710 — Weimar, Germany
DEATH: July, 1, 1784 — Berlin, Germany
TEACHER(S): J.S. Bach, Graun
COMPOSITIONAL MEDIA: orchestra, chamber music,
keyboard, choral
ITEMS OF INTEREST: eldest son of J.S. Bach

Bacharach, Burt

BIRTH: May 12, 1928 — Kansas City, MO
TEACHER(S): Milhaud, Martinu, Cowell
COMPOSITIONAL MEDIA: songs, film and/or T.V.
ITEMS OF INTEREST: best known works include "Raindrops Keep
Falling on My Head," "Do You Know the Way to San Jose," "What
the World Needs Now Is Love"

Bacon, Ernst

BIRTH: May 26, 1898 — Chicago, IL   DEATH: March 16, 1990
TEACHER(S): Oldberg, Bloch, Goossens
COMPOSITIONAL MEDIA: orchestra, chamber music, choral,
opera, theatrical
ITEMS OF INTEREST: teacher — Converse College, SC and
Syracuse University,NY; Pulitzer Prize 1932

Balakirev, Mily Alexeievich (Ba la' ki rev)

BIRTH: January 2, 1837 — Nizhny-Novgorod
DEATH: May 29, 1910 — St. Petersburg
TEACHER(S): his mother, Dubuque
COMPOSITIONAL MEDIA: orchestra, chamber music, keyboard,
choral, songs
ITEMS OF INTEREST: taught Cui, Rimsky-Korsakov, Borodin,
Mussorgsky

Barber, Samuel

BIRTH: March 9, 1910 — West Chester, PA
DEATH: January 23, 1981 — New York, NY
TEACHER(S): Scalero
COMPOSITIONAL MEDIA: orchestra, chamber music, keyboard, opera, songs
ITEMS OF INTEREST: teacher — Curtis Institute, best known works include orchestral work "Adagio for Strings"

Bartók, Béla

BIRTH: March 25, 1881 — Transylvania
DEATH: September 26, 1945 — New York
TEACHER(S): Koessler, L. Erkel
COMPOSITIONAL MEDIA: orchestra, chamber music, ballet, keyboard, choral
ITEMS OF INTEREST: collected Hungarian folk music with Kodaly; teacher — Royal Academy of Music, Budapest; best known works include "Concerto for Orchestra"

Bassett, Leslie

BIRTH: January 22, 1923 — Hanford, CA
TEACHER(S): Finney, Honegger, N. Boulanger, Gerhard, Davidovsky
COMPOSITIONAL MEDIA: orchestra, chamber music, keyboard, choral, electronic
ITEMS OF INTEREST: teacher — University of Michigan

Beethoven, Ludwig van

BIRTH: December 16, 1770 — Bonn, Germany
DEATH: March 26, 1827 — Vienna, Austria
TEACHER(S): his father, Neefe, Haydn, Schenk, Salieri, Albrechtsberger

COMPOSITIONAL MEDIA: orchestra, chamber music, keyboard, choral, opera

ITEMS OF INTEREST: one of the most important composers of all times, very prolific, hearing began to fail until he became deaf (1820), continued to compose until his death

Bellini, Vincenzo

BIRTH: November 3, 1801 — Catania, Sicily
DEATH: September 23, 1835 — Puteaux, France
TEACHER(S): Zingarelli
COMPOSITIONAL MEDIA: chamber music, choral, opera
ITEMS OF INTEREST: operas very melodic, still in current repertoire; best known works include "Norma"

Bennett, Robert Russell

BIRTH: June 15, 1894—Kansas City, MO   DEATH: Aug. 17, 1981
TEACHER(S): N. Boulanger
COMPOSITIONAL MEDIA: orchestra, chamber music, keyboard, choral, opera, songs, theatrical, film, T.V., concert band
ITEMS OF INTEREST: best known works include orchestrations of Broadway musicals including "My Fair Lady"

Berg, Alban

BIRTH: February 9, 1885 — Vienna, Austria
DEATH: December 24, 1935 — Vienna, Austria
TEACHER(S): Schoenberg
COMPOSITIONAL MEDIA: orchestra, chamber music, keyboard, opera, songs
ITEMS OF INTEREST: compositions incorporate twelve tone techniques; best know works include "Wozzeck"

Berio, Luciano

BIRTH: October 24, 1925 — Oneglia, Italy
TEACHER(S): his father, Ghedini, Giulini, Dallapiccola
COMPOSITIONAL MEDIA: orchestra, chamber music, ballet, keyboard, choral, electronic
ITEMS OF INTEREST: founded (1955) — Studio di fonologia musicale, Milan, for study of electronic music; teacher — Juilliard School, NY; compositions incorporate special notation and electronic techniques

Berlin, Irving

BIRTH: May 11, 1888 — Temun, Russia   DEATH: Sept. 22, 1989
COMPOSITIONAL MEDIA: songs, theatrical, popular, film and/or T.V.
ITEMS OF INTEREST: best known works include "Alexander's Ragtime Band," "Blue Skies," "White Christmas," "God Bless America"

Berlioz, Hector (bär′ lē ohz)

BIRTH: December 11, 1803 — La-Cote-Saint-André, Isère
DEATH: March 8, 1869 — Paris
TEACHER(S): Lesueur, Reicha
COMPOSITIONAL MEDIA: orchestra, choral, opera, books
ITEMS OF INTEREST: best known works include the use of orchestral colors within compositions — exemplified in the composition "Symphonie fantastique"

Bernstein, Leonard

BIRTH: Aug. 25, 1918 — Lawrence, MA   DEATH: Oct. 14, 1990
TEACHER(S): Piston, Hill, R. Thompson
COMPOSITIONAL MEDIA: orchestra, chamber music, ballet, keyboard, choral, opera, songs, theatrical, film, T.V., books
ITEMS OF INTEREST: conductor — New York City Center 1945-48, New York Philharmonic 1958-68; guest conductor and lec-

turer throughout the world who helped bring the knowledge and appreciation of classical music to the masses

Billings, William

BIRTH: October 7, 1746   Boston, MA
DEATH: September 26, 1800 — Boston, MA
TEACHER(S): self-taught
COMPOSITIONAL MEDIA: choral
ITEMS OF INTEREST: published collections of choral music for the church

Bizet, Georges (bē zā')

BIRTH: October 25, 1838 — Paris, France
DEATH: June 3, 1875 — Bougival, France
TEACHER(S): Halévy
COMPOSITIONAL MEDIA: orchestra, keyboard, choral, opera, songs, theatrical
ITEMS OF INTEREST: best known works include the opera "Carmen"

Bloch, Ernest

BIRTH: July 24, 1880 — Geneva, Switzerland
DEATH: July 15, 1959 — Portland, OR
TEACHER(S): Jaques-Dalcroze, Ysaye, I. Knorr, Thuille
COMPOSITIONAL MEDIA: orchestra, chamber music, keyboard, opera
ITEMS OF INTEREST: teacher — in Geneva, University of California/Berkeley; Director — Cleveland Institute, San Francisco Conservatory; pupils included Sessions, Porter, Jacobi, Freed, Stevens, Bernard Rogers

Blow, John

BIRTH: February 23, 1649 — Nottinghamshire
DEATH: October 1, 1708 — Westminster, London

TEACHER(S): Cooke, Gibbons
COMPOSITIONAL MEDIA: keyboard, choral, songs, opera
ITEMS OF INTEREST: organist at Westminster Abbey, pupils included Purcell

Boccherini, Luigi (bok kā rē′ nē)

BIRTH: February 19, 1743 — Lucca
DEATH: May 28, 1805 — Madrid
TEACHER(S): Vanucci
COMPOSITIONAL MEDIA: orchestra, chamber music, choral, opera
ITEMS OF INTEREST: professional cellist

Bolcom, William

BIRTH: May 26, 1938 — Seattle, WA
TEACHER(S): McKay, Verrall, Milhaud, Rivier, Messiaen, L. Smith
COMPOSITIONAL MEDIA: chamber music, keyboard, opera, electronic, popular
ITEMS OF INTEREST: teacher — University of Michigan, authority on American popular music from the 1900's

Borodin, Alexander Porfirievich (boh roh dēn′)

BIRTH: November 12, 1833 — St. Petersburg, Russia
DEATH: February 28, 1887 — St. Petersburg, Russia
COMPOSITIONAL MEDIA: orchestra, chamber music, keyboard, opera, songs
ITEMS OF INTEREST: associate of Balakirev, Stasov, Mussorgsky

Boulanger, Lili (boo lahn zhā′)

BIRTH: August 21, 1893 — Paris, France
DEATH: March 15, 1918 — Mezy, France
COMPOSITIONAL MEDIA: orchestra, chamber music, choral, songs
ITEMS OF INTEREST: sister of Nadia Boulanger

Boulanger, Nadia

BIRTH: September 16, 1887 — Paris, France
DEATH: October 22, 1979 — Paris, France
TEACHER(S): Faure, Widor
COMPOSITIONAL MEDIA: orchestra, keyboard, choral
ITEMS OF INTEREST: teacher — American Conservatory,
Fontainebleau; pupils included Carter, Copland, Harris, Piston, other
well-known American and European composers

Boulez, Pierre (bōō lĕz')

BIRTH: March 26, 1925 — Montbrison, France
TEACHER(S): Messiaen, Leibowitz
COMPOSITIONAL MEDIA: orchestra, chamber music, keyboard,
books
ITEMS OF INTEREST: conductor — Cleveland Orchestra, B.B.C.
Orchestra, New York Philharmonic; leader in developing and pro-
moting serialism and other contemporary music techniques

Brahms, Johannes

BIRTH: May 7, 1833 — Hamburg, Germany
DEATH: April 3, 1897 — Vienna, Austria
TEACHER(S): Eduard Marxsen
COMPOSITIONAL MEDIA: orchestra, chamber music, keyboard,
choral, songs
ITEMS OF INTEREST: close associate of Robert and Clara
Schumann; although a romantic composer, his compositions
reflected a great understanding and love for classical style

Britten, Benjamin

BIRTH: November 22, 1913 — Lowestoft, England
DEATH: December 4, 1976 — Aldeburgh, England
TEACHER(S): Bridge, Ireland
COMPOSITIONAL MEDIA: orchestra, chamber music, choral,

opera, songs
ITEMS OF INTEREST: his "The Young Person's Guide to the Orchestra" has introduced the medium to children throughout the world

Brown, Earle

BIRTH: December 26, 1926 — Lunenburg, MA
TEACHER(S): highly trained in the Schillinger system
COMPOSITIONAL MEDIA: chamber music, keyboard, electronic
ITEMS OF INTEREST: associated with Cage and Tudor, compositions incorporate aleatoric techniques

Brubeck, Dave

BIRTH: December 6, 1920 — Concord, CA
TEACHER(S): Milhaud, Schoenberg
COMPOSITIONAL MEDIA: orchestra, chamber music, choral, songs, jazz
ITEMS OF INTEREST: incorporated classical techniques and various time signatures in jazz, best known works include "Take Five," "Blue Rondo A La Turk"

Bruch, Max

BIRTH: January 6, 1838 — Cologne, Germany
DEATH: October 2, 1920 — Friednau, Germany
TEACHER(S): F. Hiller, Reinecke
COMPOSITIONAL MEDIA: orchestra, chamber music, keyboard, choral, opera, songs
ITEMS OF INTEREST: teacher — Berlin Academy

Bruckner, Anton

BIRTH: September 4, 1824 — Ansfelden, Austria
DEATH: October 11, 1896 — Vienna, Austria
TEACHER(S): Sechter
COMPOSITIONAL MEDIA: orchestra, chamber music, keyboard, choral

ITEMS OF INTEREST: teacher — Vienna Conservatory, Vienna University

Burgmüller, Friedrich Johann Franz

BIRTH: December 4, 1806 — Regensburg
DEATH: February 13, 1874 — Beaulieu, France
COMPOSITIONAL MEDIA: ballet, keyboard, songs
ITEMS OF INTEREST: probably most famous for his piano pieces which are a standard in pedagogical literature

Burke, Johnny

BIRTH: October 3, 1908 — Antioch, CA
DEATH: February 25, 1964 — New York, NY
COMPOSITIONAL MEDIA: songs, popular
ITEMS OF INTEREST: best known works include "What's New," "Pennies from Heaven," "And the Angels Sing"

Burns, Ralph

BIRTH: June 29, 1922 — Newton, MA
TEACHER(S): Deviney
COMPOSITIONAL MEDIA: songs, theatrical, popular
ITEMS OF INTEREST: best known works include "Early Autumn" and arranging Broadway musicals — "No Strings," "Funny Girls"

Busoni, Ferruccio

BIRTH: April 1, 1866 — Empoli, Italy
DEATH: July 27, 1924 — Berlin, Germany
COMPOSITIONAL MEDIA: orchestra, chamber music, keyboard, opera, books
ITEMS OF INTEREST: published critical, theoretical, and literary works, anticipating developments in 20th-century music

Buxtehude, Dietrich

BIRTH: 1637 — Oldelsloe, Holstein
DEATH: May 9, 1707 — Lübeck, Germany
TEACHER(S): his father
COMPOSITIONAL MEDIA: chamber music, keyboard, choral
ITEMS OF INTEREST: influenced J.S. Bach

Byrd, William

BIRTH: 1543 — Lincolnshire, England
DEATH: July 4, 1623 — Stondon, England
COMPOSITIONAL MEDIA: choral, songs
ITEMS OF INTEREST: organist — Lincoln Cathedral, Chapel Royal

C

Caccini, Giulio (kahtch chē′ nē)

BIRTH: 1545 — Tivoli, Italy
DEATH: December 10, 1618 — Florence, Italy
COMPOSITIONAL MEDIA: choral, opera
ITEMS OF INTEREST: composed the opera "L'Euridice", 1600

Cage, John

BIRTH: Sept. 5, 1912 — Los Angeles   DEATH: August 12, 1992
TEACHER(S): Weiss, Cowell, Schoenberg
COMPOSITIONAL MEDIA: orchestra, keyboard
ITEMS OF INTEREST: compositions incorporate prepared piano,
tape, aleatory techniques

Cambini, Giuseppe Maria Gioacchino

BIRTH: February 13, 1746 — Livorno
DEATH: December 29, 1825 — Bicêtre, Paris
TEACHER(S): Padre Martini
COMPOSITIONAL MEDIA: orchestra, chamber music, ballet, organ, choral, opera
ITEMS OF INTEREST: died in the poor house

Carissimi, Giacomo

BIRTH: April 18, 1605 — Marino, Italy
DEATH: January 12, 1674 — Rome, Italy
COMPOSITIONAL MEDIA: choral
ITEMS OF INTEREST: Choir Master at San Apollinare, Rome

Carse, Adam von Ahn

BIRTH: May 19, 1878 — Newcastle-on-Tyne, England
DEATH: November 2, 1958 — Buckingham, England
TEACHER(S): Corder, Burnett
COMPOSITIONAL MEDIA: orchestra, chamber music, keyboard, choral, songs, books
ITEMS OF INTEREST: teacher — Winchester College, Royal Academy of Music

Carter, Benny

BIRTH: August 8, 1907 — New York, NY
COMPOSITIONAL MEDIA: popular, jazz, film and/or T.V.
ITEMS OF INTEREST: best known works include jazz compositions — "When Lights Are Low," "Harlem Mood;" TV score — "M Squad"

Carter, Elliott

BIRTH: December 11, 1908 — New York, NY

TEACHER(S): Piston, Hill, N. Boulanger
COMPOSITIONAL MEDIA: orchestra, chamber music, ballet, keyboard, choral, opera, songs
ITEMS OF INTEREST: teacher — Juilliard, Columbia, Yale, Cornell, M.I.T.; music critic as well as a composer

Casadesus, Robert

BIRTH: April 7, 1899 — Paris, France
DEATH: September 19, 1972 — Paris, France
TEACHER(S): Leroux
COMPOSITIONAL MEDIA: orchestra, chamber music, keyboard,
ITEMS OF INTEREST: teacher — American Conservatory/Fontainebleau

Casals, Pablo (käh sähls´)

BIRTH: December 29, 1876 — Vendrell, Spain
DEATH: October 22, 1973 — Puerto Rico
COMPOSITIONAL MEDIA: chamber music, choral
ITEMS OF INTEREST: professional cellist

Casella, Alfredo

BIRTH: July 25, 1883 — Turin, France
DEATH: March 5, 1947 — Rome, Italy
TEACHER(S): Leroux, Faure
COMPOSITIONAL MEDIA: orchestra, chamber music, ballet, keyboard, choral, opera, books
ITEMS OF INTEREST: professional pianist, conductor

Chaminade, Cécile (shäh mē nähd´)

BIRTH: August 8, 1857 — Paris, France
DEATH: April 18, 1944 — Monte Carlo, France
TEACHER(S): Godard

COMPOSITIONAL MEDIA: orchestra, keyboard, choral, songs
ITEMS OF INTEREST: professional pianist

Chávez, Carlos (chăh′ vāz)

BIRTH: June 13, 1899 — Mexico City
DEATH: August 2, 1978 — Mexico City
TEACHER(S): Ponce, J.B. Fuentes
COMPOSITIONAL MEDIA: orchestra, chamber music, ballet,
keyboard, opera, songs, books
ITEMS OF INTEREST: probably most famous Mexican composer

Cherubini, Luigi (kā roo bē′ nē)

BIRTH: September 14, 1760 — Florence, Italy
DEATH: March 13, 1842 — Paris, France
TEACHER(S): his father, Sarti
COMPOSITIONAL MEDIA: orchestra, chamber music, ballet,
keyboard, choral, opera, books
ITEMS OF INTEREST: developed dramatic style of French opera

Chihara, Paul

BIRTH: July 9, 1938 — Seattle, WA
TEACHER(S): N. Boulanger, Schuller, Palmer, Pepping
COMPOSITIONAL MEDIA: orchestra, chamber music, ballet, choral,
electronic, film
ITEMS OF INTEREST: teacher — University of California/Los
Angeles

Childs, Barney

BIRTH: February 13, 1926 — Spokane, WA
TEACHER(S): Chávez, Copland, Carter
COMPOSITIONAL MEDIA: orchestra, chamber music, choral
ITEMS OF INTEREST: compositions include aleatory techniques,
American Indian melodies

Chopin, Fréderic (shŏ pǎn')

BIRTH: February 22, 1810 — Zelazowa Wola, Poland
DEATH: October 17, 1849 — Paris, France
TEACHER(S): his father, Elsner
COMPOSITIONAL MEDIA: orchestra, keyboard, songs
ITEMS OF INTEREST: taught piano privately, professional pianist, best known works include his piano compositions

Chou, Wen-chung

BIRTH: June 29, 1923 — Chefoo, China
TEACHER(S): Varèse, Luening, McKinley, Slonimsky, Martinu
COMPOSITIONAL MEDIA: orchestra, chamber music, keyboard, film
ITEMS OF INTEREST: teacher — Columbia University

Cimarosa, Domenico (chē mah rŏh' sah)

BIRTH: December 17, 1749 — Aversa, Italy
DEATH: January 11, 1801 — Venice, Italy
TEACHER(S): Sacchini
COMPOSITIONAL MEDIA: chamber music, keyboard, choral, opera, songs
ITEMS OF INTEREST: very prolific opera composer

Clarke, Jeremiah

BIRTH: 1673 — London, England
DEATH: December 1, 1707 — London, England
COMPOSITIONAL MEDIA: harpsichord, choral, opera, songs, theatrical
ITEMS OF INTEREST: he committed suicide

Clementi, Muzio

BIRTH: January 23, 1752 — Rome, Italy
DEATH: March 10, 1832 — Evesham, England

TEACHER(S): Buroni, Condiceli, Carponi
COMPOSITIONAL MEDIA: orchestra, keyboard, books
ITEMS OF INTEREST: professional pianist

Coleman, Cy

BIRTH: June 14, 1929 — New York, NY
TEACHER(S): Gruen, Marcus
COMPOSITIONAL MEDIA: songs, theatrical, popular
ITEMS OF INTEREST: best known works include scores to
Broadway musicals — "Barnum," "Wildcat," "Sweet Charity"

Colgrass, Michael

BIRTH: April 22, 1932 — Chicago, IL
TEACHER(S): Milhaud, Foss, Riegger, Weber
COMPOSITIONAL MEDIA: orchestra, chamber music, choral
ITEMS OF INTEREST: percussionist who began compositional
career composing for that medium, Pulitzer Prize winner

Copland, Aaron

BIRTH: November 14, 1900 — Brooklyn, NY
DEATH: December 2, 1990 — Westchester, NY
COMPOSITIONAL MEDIA: orchestra, chamber music, ballet,
keyboard, choral, opera, jazz, film and/or T.V., books
ITEMS OF INTEREST: very popular American composer;
compositions incorporate American folk music, jazz, and serial
techniques; Pulitzer Prize winner

Corelli, Arcangelo

BIRTH: February 17, 1653 — Fusignano, Italy
DEATH: January 8, 1713 — Rome, Italy
TEACHER(S): Benvenuti, Simonelli
COMPOSITIONAL MEDIA: orchestra, chamber music

ITEMS OF INTEREST: developed the baroque sonata and concerto grosso

Corigliano, John

BIRTH: February 16, 1938 — New York
TEACHER(S): Leuning, Giannini, Crestor
COMPOSITIONAL MEDIA: orchestra, chamber music, choral, electronic, theatrical
ITEMS OF INTEREST: teacher — Liehman College, NY; arranged Bizet's "Carmen" for rock group and synthesizer — "The Naked Carmen"

Couperin, Francois (koo pŭ ran')

BIRTH: November 10, 1668 — Paris
DEATH: September 12, 1733 — Paris
TEACHER(S): Charles Couperin (his father)
COMPOSITIONAL MEDIA: chamber music, keyboard, choral, books
ITEMS OF INTEREST: his book on harpsichord playing, "L'art de toucher la clavecin" 1717, is a standard in pedagogical literature

Cowell, Henry

BIRTH: March 11, 1897 — Menlo Park, CA
DEATH: December 10, 1965 — Shady, NY
TEACHER(S): Hornbostel, Woodman, Buhlig
COMPOSITIONAL MEDIA: orchestra, chamber music, ballet, keyboard, choral, opera, songs, books
ITEMS OF INTEREST: promoter of contemporary American music; compositions incorporate tone clusters, playing on the inside of the piano, aleatoric techniques

Creston, Paul

BIRTH: October 10, 1906 — New York
DEATH: August 24, 1985 — San Diego, CA

TEACHER(S): Randegger, Dethier, Yon
COMPOSITIONAL MEDIA: orchestra, chamber music, keyboard, choral, books
ITEMS OF INTEREST: teacher — Central Washington State College

Crüger, Johann

BIRTH: April 9, 1598 — Gross-Breese, Prussia
DEATH: February 23, 1662 — Berlin, Germany
TEACHER(S): Homberger
COMPOSITIONAL MEDIA: choral, books
ITEMS OF INTEREST: best known works include chorale melody "Nun danket alle Gott"

Crumb, George

BIRTH: October 24, 1929 — Charleston, WV
TEACHER(S): Blacher, Finney
COMPOSITIONAL MEDIA: orchestra, chamber music, keyboard, choral, songs, electronic
ITEMS OF INTEREST: teacher — University of Colorado, State University of New York/Buffalo, University of Pennsylvania

Cui, Cesar Antonovich (kwē)

BIRTH: January 18, 1835 — Vilna, Russia
DEATH: March 26, 1918 — Petrograd, Russia
TEACHER(S): Moniuszko
COMPOSITIONAL MEDIA: orchestra, chamber music, keyboard, choral, opera, songs, books
ITEMS OF INTEREST: worked with Balakirev, was music critic

Czerny, Carl (chär' nē)

BIRTH: February 20, 1791 — Vienna, Austria
DEATH: July 15, 1857 — Vienna, Austria
TEACHER(S): his father, Beethoven

COMPOSITIONAL MEDIA: orchestra, chamber music, keyboard, choral

ITEMS OF INTEREST: pupils included Liszt; his keyboard pedagogy exercises are a standard in pedagogical literature

D

Dahl, Ingolf

BIRTH: June 9, 1912 — Hamburg, Germany
DEATH: August 7, 1970 — Frutigen, Switzerland
TEACHER(S): Jarnach, N. Boulanger
COMPOSITIONAL MEDIA: orchestra, chamber music, keyboard, choral
ITEMS OF INTEREST: teacher — University of Southern California

Dalcroze, Émile-Jaques (dähl krŏhz′)

BIRTH: July 6, 1865 — Vienna, Austria
DEATH: July 1, 1950 — Geneva, Switzerland
TEACHER(S): R. Fuchs, Fauré, Bruckner, Delibes
COMPOSITIONAL MEDIA: orchestra, chamber music, keyboard, choral, opera, songs, theatrical, books
ITEMS OF INTEREST: teacher — Geneva Conservatory; developed eurhythmics, a system for teaching rhythm through movement

Dallapiccola, Luigi

BIRTH: February 3, 1904 — Pisino, Italy
DEATH: February 19,1975 — Florence, Italy
TEACHER(S): Consolo, Frazzi
COMPOSITIONAL MEDIA: orchestra, chamber music, keyboard, choral, opera, songs,
ITEMS OF INTEREST: compositions incorporate twelve-tone techniques

Damrosch, Walter Johannes

BIRTH: January 30, 1862 — Breslau, Germany
DEATH: December 22, 1950 — New York, NY
TEACHER(S): Leopold Damrosch (his father), Draeseke, Rischbieter
COMPOSITIONAL MEDIA: choral, opera, songs, theatrical
ITEMS OF INTEREST: conductor — Metropolitan Opera House, New York Philharmonic, N.B.C. Symphony Orchestra

Davidovsky, Mario

BIRTH: March 4, 1934 — Buenos Aires, Argentina
TEACHER(S): Epstein
COMPOSITIONAL MEDIA: orchestra, chamber music, keyboard, electronic
ITEMS OF INTEREST: assistant director — Columbia-Princeton Electronic Music Center

Davies, Peter Maxwell

BIRTH: September 8, 1934 — Manchester, England
TEACHER(S): Petrassi, Sessions
COMPOSITIONAL MEDIA: orchestra, chamber music, keyboard, choral, opera, electronic, theatrical
ITEMS OF INTEREST: worked for more performance of contemporary music in England

Debussy, Claude (dĕh′ bü sē)

BIRTH: August 22, 1862 — Saint-Germain-en-Laye, France
DEATH: March 25, 1918 — Paris, France
TEACHER(S): Marmontel, Lavignac, Guiraud, Franck
COMPOSITIONAL MEDIA: orchestra, chamber music, ballet,
keyboard, choral, opera, songs, books
ITEMS OF INTEREST: along with Ravel was the premier composer
in the Impressionist style, worked closely with French symbolist poets

Delibes, Léo (dŭ lēb′)

BIRTH: February 21, 1836 — St. Germain-du-Val, France
DEATH: January 16, 1891 — Paris, France
TEACHER(S): Adam
COMPOSITIONAL MEDIA: ballet, choral, opera, songs
ITEMS OF INTEREST: teacher — Paris Conservatory

Delius, Frederick

BIRTH: January 29, 1862 — Bradford, England
DEATH: June 10, 1934 — Grez-sur-Loing, France
TEACHER(S): Reinecke, Jadassohn
COMPOSITIONAL MEDIA: orchestra, chamber music, choral,
opera, songs
ITEMS OF INTEREST: best known for stage works

Dello Joio, Norman

BIRTH: January 24, 1913 — New York, NY
TEACHER(S): Yon, Wagenaar, Hindemith
COMPOSITIONAL MEDIA: orchestra, chamber music, keyboard,
choral, opera, concert band
ITEMS OF INTEREST: teacher — Sarah Lawrence
College, Mannes College, Boston University

Del Tredici, David

BIRTH: March 16, 1937 — Cloverdale, CA
TEACHER(S): A. Elston, Shifrin, Sessions, Kim, Milhaud
COMPOSITIONAL MEDIA: orchestra, chamber music, keyboard,
choral, songs
ITEMS OF INTEREST: teacher — Harvard University, Boston
University

des Prez, Josquin

BIRTH: 1450 — Beaurevoir, France
DEATH: August 27, 1521 — Conde-sur-l'Escaut, France
TEACHER(S): Okeghem
COMPOSITIONAL MEDIA: chamber music, choral
ITEMS OF INTEREST: established the standard of polyphonic writing
by which other composers of the 16th century were judged

Diabelli, Anton

BIRTH: September 5, 1781 — Mattsee, Germany
DEATH: April 8, 1858 — Vienna, Austria
TEACHER(S): Michael Haydn
COMPOSITIONAL MEDIA: chamber music, ballet, keyboard,
choral, opera, songs
ITEMS OF INTEREST: composed a waltz theme on which
Beethoven based his "Diabelli Variations"

Diamond, David

BIRTH: July 9, 1915 — Rochester, NY
TEACHER(S): Rogers, Sessions, N. Boulanger
COMPOSITIONAL MEDIA: orchestra, chamber music, ballet,
keyboard, choral, songs
ITEMS OF INTEREST: teacher — Manhattan School

Dittersdorf, Karl Ditters von

BIRTH: November 2, 1739 — Vienna, Austria
DEATH: October 24, 1799 — Castle Rothlhotta, Bohemia
TEACHER(S): König, Ziegler, Trani, Bono
COMPOSITIONAL MEDIA: orchestra, chamber music, ballet, keyboard, choral, opera
ITEMS OF INTEREST: succeeded Michael Haydn as kapellmeister to Bishop of Grosswardein, Hungary

Donizetti, Gaetano (doh nē tset′ tē)

BIRTH: November 29, 1797 — Bergamo, Italy
DEATH: April 8, 1848 — Bergamo, Italy
TEACHER(S): Mayr
COMPOSITIONAL MEDIA: chamber music, keyboard, choral, opera
ITEMS OF INTEREST: best known works include opera "Lucia di Lamermoor"

Dowland, John

BIRTH: December 1562 — near Dublin, England
DEATH: January 21, 1626 — London, England
COMPOSITIONAL MEDIA: songs
ITEMS OF INTEREST: professional lutenist who mainly composed for his instrument

Druckman, Jacob

BIRTH: June 6, 1928 — Philadelphia, PA
TEACHER(S): B. Wagenaar, Persichetti, Mennin, Copland
COMPOSITIONAL MEDIA: orchestra, chamber music, choral, electronic
ITEMS OF INTEREST: teacher — various colleges in New York area, associate — Columbia-Princeton Electronic Music Center

Dufay, Guillaume (dü fäh′ ē)

BIRTH: 1400 — Hainault, Burgundy
DEATH: November 27, 1474 — Cambrai, France
TEACHER(S): Loquevielle, Grenon
COMPOSITIONAL MEDIA: choral
ITEMS OF INTEREST: composed polyphonic music in both sacred and secular styles

Dukas, Paul (dü käh′)

BIRTH: October 1, 1865 — Paris, France
DEATH: May 17, 1935 — Paris, France
TEACHER(S): Mathias, Dubois, Guirraud
COMPOSITIONAL MEDIA: orchestra, chamber music, keyboard, opera
ITEMS OF INTEREST: best known works include "Sorcerer's Apprentice"

Duke, Vernon

BIRTH: October 10, 1903 — Parfianovka, Russia
DEATH: January 16, 1969 — Santa Monica, CA
TEACHER(S): Glière
COMPOSITIONAL MEDIA: orchestra, chamber music, ballet, keyboard, choral, popular
ITEMS OF INTEREST: settled in the US — 1929, popular songs included "April in Paris"

Dumont, Henri (dü mon′)

BIRTH: 1610 — Villers-l'Evèque, France
DEATH: May 8, 1684 — Paris, France
COMPOSITIONAL MEDIA: chamber music, choral
ITEMS OF INTEREST: organist — Church of St. Paul, Paris

Dunstable, John

BIRTH: 1390 — Dunstable, England
DEATH: December 24, 1453 — London, England
COMPOSITIONAL MEDIA: choral
ITEMS OF INTEREST: served Duke John, brother of King Henry V

Dupré, Marcel (du prā´)

BIRTH: May 3, 1886 — Rouen, France
DEATH: May 30, 1971 — Meudon, France
TEACHER(S): his father, Guilmant, Widor
COMPOSITIONAL MEDIA: organ, choral
ITEMS OF INTEREST: toured as an organist; teacher — Paris
Conservatory, American Conservatory in Fontainebleau

Dussek, Jan Ladislav (dū´ sek)

BIRTH: February 12, 1760 — Caslav, Bohemia
DEATH: March 20, 1812 — St-Germain-en-Laye
TEACHER(S): Spenar, K.Ph.E. Bach
COMPOSITIONAL MEDIA: chamber music, keyboard
ITEMS OF INTEREST: best known works include piano writing

Dvořák, Antonin (dvŏhr´ zhahk)

BIRTH: September 8, 1841 — Muhlhausen, Bohemia
DEATH: May 1, 1904 — Prague, Czechoslovakia
TEACHER(S): Pitzsch
COMPOSITIONAL MEDIA: orchestra, chamber music, keyboard,
choral, opera, songs
ITEMS OF INTEREST: teacher — Prague Conservatory; director of
National Conservatory, New York; best known works include "New
World Symphony"

Dylan, Bob

BIRTH: May 24, 1941 — Duluth, MN

COMPOSITIONAL MEDIA: songs, popular
ITEMS OF INTEREST: real name is Bob Zimmerman; best known
works include folk music of '60s — "Blowin' in the Wind;" compositions in the '80s of a more spiritual nature

E

Eccles, John

BIRTH: 1668 — London, England
DEATH: January 12, 1735 — Kingston-on-Thames, England
TEACHER(S): Solomon Eccles (his father)
COMPOSITIONAL MEDIA: chamber music, songs, theatrical, books
ITEMS OF INTEREST: professional violinist, member of the Queen's
band

Effinger, Cecil

BIRTH: July 22, 1914—Colorado Springs, CO   DEATH: Dec. 22, 1990
TEACHER(S): B. Wagenaar, N. Boulanger
COMPOSITIONAL MEDIA: orchestra, chamber music, organ,
choral, opera, concert band
ITEMS OF INTEREST: teacher — University of Colorado

El-Dabh, Halim

BIRTH: March 4, 1921 — Cairo, Egypt
TEACHER(S): Fine, Copland
COMPOSITIONAL MEDIA: orchestra, ballet, electronic
ITEMS OF INTEREST: teacher — Kent State University, compositions incorporate Egyptian musical materials

Elgar, Edward

BIRTH: June 2, 1857 — Broadheath, England
DEATH: February 23, 1934 — Worcester, England
TEACHER(S): his father
COMPOSITIONAL MEDIA: orchestra, chamber music, choral, songs, theatrical
ITEMS OF INTEREST: probably most most famous for "Pomp and Circumstance"

Ellington, Edward Kennedy (Duke)

BIRTH: April 29, 1899 — Washington, DC
DEATH: May 24, 1974 — New York, NY
COMPOSITIONAL MEDIA: orchestra, chamber music, choral, songs, popular, jazz
ITEMS OF INTEREST: probably the most famous jazz composer of the 1900's — "Satin Doll," "Sophisticated Lady," "Do Nothin' Till You Hear from Me"

Enesco, Georges

BIRTH: August 19, 1881 — Rumania
DEATH: May 4, 1955 — Paris, France
TEACHER(S): Fauré, Massenet, Dubois, Gédalge, Thomas
COMPOSITIONAL MEDIA: orchestra, chamber music, keyboard, choral, opera
ITEMS OF INTEREST: professional violinist, pupils included Yehudi Menuhin

Erb, Donald

BIRTH: January 17, 1927 — Youngstown, OH
TEACHER(S): Gaburo, Heiden, M. Dick, N. Boulanger
COMPOSITIONAL MEDIA: orchestra, chamber music, keyboard, choral, electronic, rock, concert band
ITEMS OF INTEREST: teacher — Electronic Music Studio, Cleveland Institute; compositions incorporate serial, aleatory techniques

Escobar, Luis Antonio

BIRTH: July 14, 1925 — Villapinzón, Colombia
TEACHER(S): Nabokov, Blancher
COMPOSITIONAL MEDIA: orchestra, chamber music, ballet, keyboard, choral, opera
ITEMS OF INTEREST: compositions incorporate Spanish dance rhythms

Etler, Alvin

BIRTH: February 19, 1913 — Battle Creek, MI
DEATH: June 13, 1973 — Northampton, MA
TEACHER(S): Shepherd, Hindemith
COMPOSITIONAL MEDIA: orchestra, chamber music, choral, opera
ITEMS OF INTEREST: teacher — Smith College, Yale, Cornell, University of Illinois

Evans, Gil

BIRTH: May 13, 1912 — Toronto, Canada   DEATH: March 20, 1988
COMPOSITIONAL MEDIA: jazz
ITEMS OF INTEREST: best known works include arrangements of Miles Davis albums — "Birth of the Cool," "Porgy and Bess," "Sketches of Spain"

F

Falla, Manuel de (fäh′ yäh)

BIRTH: November 23, 1876 — Cadiz, Spain
DEATH: November 14, 1946 — Alta Gracia, Argentina
TEACHER(S): Pedrell
COMPOSITIONAL MEDIA: orchestra, chamber music, ballet, keyboard, opera, songs
ITEMS OF INTEREST: while in Paris (1907-14) worked with Debussy, Dukas, Ravel

Fauré, Gabriel (fōh rěh′)

BIRTH: May 12, 1845 — Pamiers, France
DEATH: November 4, 1924 — Paris, France
TEACHER(S): Niedermeyer, Saint-Saëns
COMPOSITIONAL MEDIA: orchestra, chamber music, keyboard, choral, opera, songs, theatrical
ITEMS OF INTEREST: teacher — Paris Conservatory; pupils included Ravel, Enescu, Schmitt, Aubert, N. Boulanger

Feldman, Morton

BIRTH: January 12, 1926—New York, NY   DEATH: Sept. 3, 1987
TEACHER(S): Riegger, Wolpe
COMPOSITIONAL MEDIA: orchestra, chamber music, choral, electronic
ITEMS OF INTEREST: worked with Cage and Brown, compositions incorporate graphic notation and experimental techniques, teacher — State University of New York/Buffalo

Fillmore, Henry

BIRTH: December 2, 1881 — Cincinnati, OH
DEATH: December 7, 1956 — Miami, FL
COMPOSITIONAL MEDIA: concert band, books
ITEMS OF INTEREST: wrote band books under the name of Harold
Bennett; best known works include "Military Escort March"

Finney, Ross Lee

BIRTH: December 23, 1906 — Wells, MN
TEACHER(S): N. Boulanger, Berg, Sessions
COMPOSITIONAL MEDIA: orchestra, chamber music, keyboard,
choral, songs
ITEMS OF INTEREST: teacher — Smith College, University
of Michigan; compositions incorporate serial techniques

Flagello, Nicholas

BIRTH: March 15, 1928 — New York, NY
TEACHER(S): Giannini, Pizzetti
COMPOSITIONAL MEDIA: orchestra, chamber music, choral,
opera, songs
ITEMS OF INTEREST: teacher — Manhattan School of Music,
Curtis Institute

Floyd, Carlisle

BIRTH: June 11, 1926 — Latta, SC
TEACHER(S): Bacon
COMPOSITIONAL MEDIA: orchestra, ballet, choral, opera, songs
ITEMS OF INTEREST: teacher — Florida State University

Foss, Lukas

BIRTH: August 15, 1922 — Berlin, Germany
TEACHER(S): N. Gallon, Scalero, R. Thompson, Hindemith

COMPOSITIONAL MEDIA: orchestra, chamber music, ballet, keyboard, choral, opera, electronic, theatrical
ITEMS OF INTEREST: settled in U.S. in 1937; pianist, teacher, conductor; founder and director — Center for Creative and Performing Arts at State University of New York/Buffalo, which is a showcase for contemporary music

Foster, Stephen Collins

BIRTH: July 4, 1826 — Lawrenceville, PA
DEATH: January 13, 1864 — New York, NY
COMPOSITIONAL MEDIA: songs
ITEMS OF INTEREST: best known works include "Old Folks at Home," "Swanee River," "Oh, Susanna!;" died penniless

Frackenpohl, Arthur

BIRTH: April 23, 1924 — Irvington, NJ
TEACHER(S): B. Rogers, Milhaud, Boulanger
COMPOSITIONAL MEDIA: orchestra, chamber music, keyboard, choral, songs, concert band, books
ITEMS OF INTEREST: teacher — State University College, Potsdam, NY

Franck, César (frahnk)

BIRTH: December 10, 1822 — Liège, Belgium
DEATH: November 8, 1890 — Paris, France
TEACHER(S): Reicha
COMPOSITIONAL MEDIA: orchestra, chamber music, keyboard, choral, opera, songs
ITEMS OF INTEREST: teacher — Paris Conservatory, pupils included d'Indy, Chausson, Bréville, Duparc, Ropartz, Vierne

Freed, Isadore

BIRTH: March 26, 1900 — Brest Litovsk, Russia
DEATH: November 10, 1960 — Rockville Center, NY
TEACHER(S): Bloch, d'Indy
COMPOSITIONAL MEDIA: orchestra, chamber music, ballet,
keyboard, choral, opera, songs
ITEMS OF INTEREST: teacher — Temple University, PA; Hartt
College of Music, Hartford, CT

Frescobaldi, Girolamo

BIRTH: September 1583 — Ferrara, Italy
DEATH: March 1, 1643 — Rome, Italy
TEACHER(S): Luzzaschi
COMPOSITIONAL MEDIA: chamber music, keyboard, choral
ITEMS OF INTEREST: of his many keyboard works, the "Toccata
and Fugue" is probably the most famous, being popular in its
transcription for orchestra

Friml, Rudolf

BIRTH: December 7, 1879 — Prague, Czechoslovakia
DEATH: November 12, 1972 — Hollywood, CA
TEACHER(S): Juranek, Foerster
COMPOSITIONAL MEDIA: operetta, film and/or T.V.
ITEMS OF INTEREST: professional piano player; best known works
include operettas "Rose Marie," "Vagabond King"

G

Gabrieli, Andrea

BIRTH: 1520 — Venice, Italy
DEATH: 1586 — Venice, Italy
TEACHER(S): Willaert
COMPOSITIONAL MEDIA: chamber music, keyboard, choral
ITEMS OF INTEREST: taught his nephew Giovanni Gabrieli, H.L.
Hassler

Gabrieli, Giovanni

BIRTH: 1554-1557 — Venice, Italy
DEATH: August 12, 1612 — Venice, Italy
TEACHER(S): Andrea Gabrieli (his uncle)
COMPOSITIONAL MEDIA: chamber music, organ, choral
ITEMS OF INTEREST: taught Schütz; famous for antiphonal writing
for two choirs situated in two different parts of the church

Gaburo, Kenneth

BIRTH: July 5, 1926 — Somerville, NJ
TEACHER(S): B. Rogers, Petrassi, B. Phillips
COMPOSITIONAL MEDIA: chamber music, keyboard, choral,
opera, songs, electronic, theatrical
ITEMS OF INTEREST: teacher — University of Illinois, University of
California/San Diego; founder — New Music Choral Ensemble

Gershwin, George

BIRTH: September 26, 1898 — Brooklyn, NY
DEATH: July 11, 1937 — Beverly Hills, CA
TEACHER(S): R. Goldmark, Cowell, Schillinger
COMPOSITIONAL MEDIA: orchestra, keyboard, theatrical, popular, jazz, film
ITEMS OF INTEREST: combined classical and jazz elements; in his short life (39 yrs.), greatly influenced the development of music; best known works include "American in Paris," "Rhapsody in Blue," and the opera "Porgy and Bess"

Giannini, Vittorio

BIRTH: October 19, 1903 — Philadelphia, PA
DEATH: November 28, 1966 — New York, NY
TEACHER(S): R. Goldmark
COMPOSITIONAL MEDIA: orchestra, chamber music, keyboard, choral, opera, songs, T.V.
ITEMS OF INTEREST: teacher — Juilliard School of Music, Manhattan School of Music, Curtis Institute; first director — North Carolina School of the Arts

Gibbons, Orlando

BIRTH: December 25, 1583 — Oxford, England
DEATH: June 5, 1625 — Canterbury, England
COMPOSITIONAL MEDIA: chamber music, choral
ITEMS OF INTEREST: organist — Chapel Royal, Westminster Abbey

Gillis, Don

BIRTH: June 17, 1912 — Cameron, MO
DEATH: January 10, 1978 — Columbia, SC
COMPOSITIONAL MEDIA: orchestra, ballet, keyboard, opera, concert band
ITEMS OF INTEREST: teacher — University of South Carolina, most famous for "Symphony #5½"

Gilmore, Patrick

BIRTH: December 25, 1829 — Co. Galway, Ireland
DEATH: September 24, 1892 — St. Louis, MO
COMPOSITIONAL MEDIA: popular, concert band
ITEMS OF INTEREST: famous band leader; best known works
include "When Johnny Comes Marching Home"

Ginastera, Alberto

BIRTH: April 11, 1916 — Buenos Aires, Argentina
DEATH: June 25, 1983
TEACHER(S): A. Palma
COMPOSITIONAL MEDIA: orchestra, chamber music, ballet,
keyboard, choral, opera, songs
ITEMS OF INTEREST: organizer and director — Center for
Advanced Musical Studies, Buenos Aires; compositions incorporate
12-tone and micro tonal techniques

Glazunov, Alexander Konstantinovich (glah zoo nohv')

BIRTH: August 10, 1865 — St. Petersburg, Russia
DEATH: March 21, 1936 — Paris, France
TEACHER(S): Rimsky-Korsakov
COMPOSITIONAL MEDIA: orchestra, chamber music, ballet,
keyboard, choral, songs
ITEMS OF INTEREST: teacher — St. Petersburg
Conservatory

Gliere, Reinhold Moritzovich

BIRTH: January 11, 1875 — Kiev, Russia
DEATH: June 23, 1956 — Moscow, Russia
TEACHER(S): Taneiev, Arensky, Ippolitov-Ivanov
COMPOSITIONAL MEDIA: orchestra, chamber music, ballet,
keyboard, opera, songs
ITEMS OF INTEREST: teacher — Moscow Conservatory; pupils in-
cluded Prokofiev, Miaskovsky

Glinka, Mikhail Ivanovich

BIRTH: June 1, 1804 — Novosspaskoye, Russia
DEATH: February 15, 1857 — Berlin, Germany
TEACHER(S): Meyer, Field
COMPOSITIONAL MEDIA: orchestra, chamber music, ballet, keyboard, choral, opera, songs, theatrical
ITEMS OF INTEREST: possibly most famous for the opera "Russlan and Ludmilla"

Gluck, Christoph Willibald

BIRTH: July 2, 1714 — Erasbach, Austria
DEATH: November 15, 1787 — Vienna, Austria
TEACHER(S): Sammartini
COMPOSITIONAL MEDIA: orchestra, chamber music, ballet, choral, opera, songs
ITEMS OF INTEREST: wrote numerous operas with the librettist Ranieri Calzabigi

Gold, Ernest

BIRTH: July 13, 1921 — Vienna, Austria
TEACHER(S): his father, Cesana
COMPOSITIONAL MEDIA: orchestra, chamber music, keyboard, film and/or T.V.
ITEMS OF INTEREST: best known works include film scores — "Exodus," "Judgement at Nuremberg"

Goldmark, Rubin

BIRTH: August 15, 1872 — New York, NY
DEATH: March 6, 1936 — New York, NY
TEACHER(S): Dvořák
COMPOSITIONAL MEDIA: orchestra, chamber music, songs
ITEMS OF INTEREST: teacher — Juilliard School of Music; pupils included Copland, Gershwin, Jacobi, Wagenaar

Goosens, Eugene

BIRTH: May 26, 1893 — London, England
DEATH: June 13, 1962 — London, England
TEACHER(S): Stanford
COMPOSITIONAL MEDIA: orchestra, chamber music, ballet, keyboard, choral, songs, theatrical
ITEMS OF INTEREST: conductor — Rochester Philharmonic, Cincinnati Symphony, Sydney Symphony

Gossec, François Joseph

BIRTH: January 17, 1734 — Vergnies, Belgium
DEATH: February 16, 1829 — Paris, France
COMPOSITIONAL MEDIA: orchestra, chamber music, ballet, choral, opera, books
ITEMS OF INTEREST: teacher — Paris Conservatory

Gottschalk, Louis Moreau

BIRTH: May 8, 1829 — New Orleans, LA
DEATH: December 18, 1869 — Rio de Janeiro, Brazil
TEACHER(S): Halle, Stamaty, Maladen
COMPOSITIONAL MEDIA: orchestra, piano, opera, songs
ITEMS OF INTEREST: professional pianist, most famous for his piano compositions

Gould, Morton

BIRTH: December 10, 1913 — Richmond Hill, NY
COMPOSITIONAL MEDIA: orchestra, chamber music, ballet, keyboard, choral, theatrical, film, concert band
ITEMS OF INTEREST: music emphasizes American themes

Gounod, Charles François

BIRTH: June 17, 1818 — Paris, France
DEATH: October 18, 1893 — Paris, France

TEACHER(S): Halévy, Lesueur, Paër, Reicha
COMPOSITIONAL MEDIA: orchestra, chamber music, keyboard, choral, opera, songs, theatrical
ITEMS OF INTEREST: best known works include the opera "Faust"

Grainger, Percy

BIRTH: July 8, 1882 — Melbourne, Australia
DEATH: February 20, 1961 — White Plains, NY
TEACHER(S): I. Knorr
COMPOSITIONAL MEDIA: orchestra, chamber music, keyboard, choral, songs, concert band
ITEMS OF INTEREST: associate of Grieg, teacher, collector of British folk songs

Gretchaninov, Alexander Tikhonovich (grĕtch ah nē′ nŏv)

BIRTH: October 25, 1864 — Moscow
DEATH: January 3, 1956 — New York
TEACHER(S): Arensky, Rimsky-Korsakov
COMPOSITIONAL MEDIA: orchestra, chamber music, keyboard, choral, opera, songs, theatrical
ITEMS OF INTEREST: settled in Paris in 1925, New York in 1939

Green, Johnny

BIRTH: October 10, 1908—New York, NY   DEATH: May 15, 1989
TEACHER(S): Spalding, Hilsberg
COMPOSITIONAL MEDIA: popular, film and/or T.V.
ITEMS OF INTEREST: best known works include "Body and Soul," "I Cover the Waterfront"

Grieg, Edvard Hagerup

BIRTH: June 15, 1843 — Bergen, Norway
DEATH: September 4, 1907 — Bergen, Norway

TEACHER(S): Moscheles, E.F.E. Richer, Hauptmann, Reinecke, Gade

COMPOSITIONAL MEDIA: orchestra, chamber music, keyboard, choral, songs, theatrical

ITEMS OF INTEREST: most famous for incidental music to Ibsen's "Peer Gynt" . . . "Peer Gynt Suites" and his piano concerto

Griffes, Charles Tomlinson

BIRTH: September 17, 1884 — Elmira, NY
DEATH: April 8, 1920 — New York, NY
TEACHER(S): Humperdinck
COMPOSITIONAL MEDIA: orchestra, chamber music, keyboard, choral, songs, theatrical
ITEMS OF INTEREST: "The White Peacock" original for piano is still popular in its orchestral version

Grofé, Ferde

BIRTH: March 27, 1892 — New York, NY
DEATH: April 3, 1972 — Santa Monica, CA
TEACHER(S): Floridia
COMPOSITIONAL MEDIA: orchestra, keyboard
ITEMS OF INTEREST: pianist and arranger for Paul Whiteman's band, best known works include the orchestral composition "Grand Canyon Suite"

Guilmant, Félix Alexandre (gēl mähn')

BIRTH: March 12, 1837 — Boulogne-sur-mer, France
DEATH: March 29, 1911 — Meudon, France
TEACHER(S): Jean-Baptiste Guilmant (his father), Lemmens
COMPOSITIONAL MEDIA: orchestra, keyboard, choral
ITEMS OF INTEREST: co-founder (with d'Indy) of Schola Cantorum

Gurlitt, Cornelius

BIRTH: February 10, 1820 — Altona, Germany
DEATH: June 17, 1901 — Altona, Germany
TEACHER(S): J.P.E. Hartmann
COMPOSITIONAL MEDIA: orchestra, chamber music, keyboard, choral, opera, songs
ITEMS OF INTEREST: teacher — Hamburg Conservatory, his piano collections are still part of today's student repertoire

H

Handel, George Frideric

BIRTH: February 23, 1685 — Halle
DEATH: April 14, 1759 — London, England
TEACHER(S): Zachow, Close
COMPOSITIONAL MEDIA: orchestra, chamber music, keyboard, choral, opera, songs
ITEMS OF INTEREST: one of the most prolific of the baroque composers; best known works include his oratorios including: "Messiah," "Israel in Egypt" and the orchestral composition "Water Music"

Harris, Roy

BIRTH: February 12, 1898—Lincoln Co., OK   DEATH: Oct. 1, 1979
TEACHER(S): Farwell, N. Boulanger
COMPOSITIONAL MEDIA: orchestra, chamber music, ballet, keyboard, choral, concert band
ITEMS OF INTEREST: teacher — several U.S. schools and colleges

Handy, William Christopher

BIRTH: November 16, 1873 — Florence, AL
DEATH: March 28, 1958 — New York, NY
COMPOSITIONAL MEDIA: popular
ITEMS OF INTEREST: father of the blues; best known works include "Memphis Blues," "St. Louis Blues"

Hanon, Charles-Louis (ah nohn')

BIRTH: July 2, 1819 — Renescure, France
DEATH: March 19, 1900 — Boulogne-sur-Mer, France
COMPOSITIONAL MEDIA: keyboard, books
ITEMS OF INTEREST: best known works include "60 Progressive Studies for Piano"

Hanson, Howard

BIRTH: October 28, 1896 — Wahoo, NE
DEATH: February 26, 1981 — Rochester, NY
TEACHER(S): Oldberg
COMPOSITIONAL MEDIA: orchestra, chamber music, ballet, keyboard, choral, opera, songs
ITEMS OF INTEREST: director — Eastman School of Music in Rochester, NY; pupils included Bergsma, Mennin, Palmer

Harrison, Lou

BIRTH: May 14, 1917 — Portland, OR
TEACHER(S): Cowell, Schoenberg
COMPOSITIONAL MEDIA: orchestra, chamber music, ballet, choral, opera, songs, theatrical
ITEMS OF INTEREST: teacher — several U.S. colleges; compositions incorporate serial, aleatory techniques, Asian instruments; built his own instruments

Hartley, Walter Sinclair

BIRTH: February 21, 1927 — Washington, DC
TEACHER(S): Hanson, Bernard Rogers
COMPOSITIONAL MEDIA: chamber music, keyboard, choral,
concert band
ITEMS OF INTEREST: teacher — State University College at
Fredonia, NY

Hassler, Hans Leo

BIRTH: October 26, 1564 — Nuremberg, Germany
DEATH: June 8, 1612 — Frankfurt, Germany
TEACHER(S): A. Gabrieli
COMPOSITIONAL MEDIA: chamber music, keyboard, choral
ITEMS OF INTEREST: best known works include his choral music
both sacred and secular

Haydn, Franz Joseph

BIRTH: March 31, 1732 — Rohrau, Austria
DEATH: May 31, 1809 — Vienna, Austria
COMPOSITIONAL MEDIA: orchestra, chamber music, keyboard,
choral, opera, songs
ITEMS OF INTEREST: very prolific output including over 100 sym-
phonies; was Kapellmeister to the Esterhazy family

Haydn, Michael

BIRTH: September 14, 1737 — Rohrau, Austria
DEATH: August 10, 1806 — Salzburg, Austria
COMPOSITIONAL MEDIA: orchestra, chamber music, keyboard,
choral, opera, songs
ITEMS OF INTEREST: brother of Joseph Haydn; succeeded
Leopold Mozart as piano teacher, Salzburg

Henderson, James Fletcher

BIRTH: December 18, 1897 — Cuthburt, GA
DEATH: December 28, 1952 — New York, NY
COMPOSITIONAL MEDIA: jazz
ITEMS OF INTEREST: probably most famous as an arranger for
Benny Goodman, Teddy Hill, the Casa Loma Orchestra

Henze, Hans Werner

BIRTH: July 1, 1926 — Gütersloh, Germany
TEACHER(S): Fortner, Leibowitz
COMPOSITIONAL MEDIA: orchestra, chamber music, ballet,
keyboard, choral, opera, songs, theatrical
ITEMS OF INTEREST: compositions incorporate twelve-tone,
microtonal, electronic techniques

Herbert, Victor

BIRTH: February 1, 1859 — Dublin, Ireland
DEATH: May 26, 1924 — New York, NY
TEACHER(S): Cossmann, Seifritz
COMPOSITIONAL MEDIA: orchestra, chamber music, keyboard,
operettas, songs, theatrical, film
ITEMS OF INTEREST: best known works include his operettas in-
cluding: "Babes in Toyland," "Naughty Marietta"

Herz, Henri

BIRTH: January 6, 1803 — Vienna, Austria
DEATH: January 5, 1888 — Paris, France
TEACHER(S): Hunten, Reicha
COMPOSITIONAL MEDIA: keyboard, books
ITEMS OF INTEREST: concert pianist, teacher — Paris
Conservatory

Hiller, Lejaren

BIRTH: February 23, 1924 — New York, NY
TEACHER(S): Sessions, Babbitt
COMPOSITIONAL MEDIA: orchestra, chamber music, keyboard, electronic
ITEMS OF INTEREST: teacher — State University of New York/Buffalo, NY; co-director — Center for the Creative and Performing Arts in Buffalo; compositions incorporate electronic, computer, visual techniques

Hindemith, Paul

BIRTH: November 16, 1895 — Hanau, Germany
DEATH: December 28, 1963 — Frankfurt, Germany
TEACHER(S): Sekles, A. Mendelssohn
COMPOSITIONAL MEDIA: orchestra, chamber music, ballet, keyboard, choral, opera, concert band, books
ITEMS OF INTEREST: settled in U.S., 1940; settled in Switzerland, 1953; neoclassical composer; teacher — Yale University, University of Zurich; compositions incorporate pan-diatonic (a theoretical approach to music in which all tones are equal)

Hodkinson, Sydney

BIRTH: January 17, 1934 — Winnipeg, Canada
TEACHER(S): Bernard Rogers, L. Mennini, Carter, Sessions, Babbitt, Bassett, Finney, Castiglioni
COMPOSITIONAL MEDIA: orchestra, chamber music, choral
ITEMS OF INTEREST: teacher — University of Michigan, Eastman School of Music; compositions incorporate serial, aleatoric, theatrical techniques

Holst, Gustav Theodore

BIRTH: September 21, 1874 — Cheltenham, England
DEATH: May 25, 1934 — London, England

TEACHER(S): Stanford
COMPOSITIONAL MEDIA: orchestra, chamber music, ballet, keyboard, opera, songs, concert band
ITEMS OF INTEREST: profession trombonist, associate of Vaughan Williams, teacher — various schools in England

Honegger, Arthur

BIRTH: March 10, 1892 — Le Havre, France
DEATH: November 27, 1955 — Paris, France
TEACHER(S): Hegar, Gedalge, Widor, d'Indy
COMPOSITIONAL MEDIA: orchestra, chamber music, ballet, keyboard, choral, opera, songs, theatrical, film, radio
ITEMS OF INTEREST: best known works include the oratorio "King David," and the orchestral composition "Pacific 231"

Hovhaness, Alan

BIRTH: March 8, 1911 — Somerville, MA
TEACHER(S): Converse, Martinu
COMPOSITIONAL MEDIA: orchestra, chamber music, keyboard, choral, opera, songs, electronic, theatrical
ITEMS OF INTEREST: teacher — Boston Conservatory; compositions incorporated
Armenian and Oriental materials, aleatoric techniques

Hummel, Johann Nepomuk

BIRTH: November 14, 1778 — Pressburg, Germany
DEATH: October 17, 1837 — Weimar, Germany
TEACHER(S): Johannes Hummel (his father), Mozart, Albrechtsberger, Salieri, Haydn
COMPOSITIONAL MEDIA: chamber music, ballet, keyboard, choral, opera, books
ITEMS OF INTEREST: Kapellmeister to Prince Esterhazy

Humperdinck, Engelbert

BIRTH: September 1, 1854 — Siegburg, Germany
DEATH: September 27, 1921 — Neustrelitz, Germany
TEACHER(S): Hiller, Gernsheim, Lachner, Rheinberger
COMPOSITIONAL MEDIA: orchestra, keyboard, choral, opera,
songs, theatrical
ITEMS OF INTEREST: assistant to Wagner at Bayreuth, best known
works include opera "Hansel and Gretel"

Husa, Karel

BIRTH: August 7, 1921 — Prague, Czechoslovakia
TEACHER(S): Řídký, Honegger, N. Boulanger
COMPOSITIONAL MEDIA: orchestra, chamber music, ballet,
keyboard, choral, concert band
ITEMS OF INTEREST: teacher — Cornell University, Pulitzer Prize
winner

I

Ibert, Jacques (ē bär′)

BIRTH: August 15, 1890 — Paris, France
DEATH: February 5, 1962 — Paris, France
TEACHER(S): Gédalge, Vidal
COMPOSITIONAL MEDIA: orchestra, chamber music, ballet,
keyboard, choral, opera, theatrical, film
ITEMS OF INTEREST: director — French Academy in Rome
1937-55

Indy, Vincent d' (dăn dē´)

BIRTH: March 27, 1851 — Paris, France
DEATH: December 2, 1931 — Paris, France
TEACHER(S): Franck
COMPOSITIONAL MEDIA: orchestra, chamber music, keyboard, choral, songs, theatrical, books
ITEMS OF INTEREST: co-founded Schola Cantorum with Bordes and Guilmant, teacher — Paris Conservatory

Ireland, John

BIRTH: August 13, 1879 — Inglewood, England
DEATH: June 12, 1962 — Washington, England
TEACHER(S): Stanford
COMPOSITIONAL MEDIA: orchestra, chamber music, keyboard, choral, songs
ITEMS OF INTEREST: teacher — Royal College of Music, pupils included Britten

Ives, Charles

BIRTH: October 20, 1874 — Danbury, CT
DEATH: May 19, 1954 — New York, NY
TEACHER(S): George Ives (his father), Horatio Parker
COMPOSITIONAL MEDIA: orchestra, chamber music, keyboard, choral, songs, books
ITEMS OF INTEREST: insurance agent by profession; compositions incorporated complex rhythms, polytonality, tone clusters, aleatoric techniques; Pulitzer Prize winner; best known works include chamber orchestra pieces "Central Park in the Dark," "The Unanswered Question," "Three Places in New England;" organ composition "Variations on American;" and piano piece "Concord Sonata"

J

Jacob, Gordon
BIRTH: July 5, 1895 — London, England   DEATH: June 8, 1984
TEACHER(S): Stanford, Vaughan Williams, Howells
COMPOSITIONAL MEDIA: orchestra, chamber music, ballet, songs,
theatrical, film
ITEMS OF INTEREST: teacher — Royal College of Music

Janácek, Leos (yah' näh chĕk)
BIRTH: July 3, 1854 — Hukvaldy, Moravia
DEATH: August 12, 1928 — Ostrau, Czechoslovakia
TEACHER(S): Skuhersky, Grill, Krenn
COMPOSITIONAL MEDIA: orchestra, chamber music, keyboard,
choral, opera
ITEMS OF INTEREST: teacher — Brno Conservatory; compositions
incorporate impressionistic techniques

Jaques-Dalcroze — see Dalcroze, Jaques

Jarnach, Philipp
BIRTH: July 26, 1892 — Noisy, France   DEATH: Dec. 17, 1982
TEACHER(S): Lavignac
COMPOSITIONAL MEDIA: orchestra, chamber music, keyboard,
choral, songs
ITEMS OF INTEREST: teacher — Cologne Conservatory, associate
of Busoni

Johnston, Ben

BIRTH: March 15, 1926 — Macon, GA
TEACHER(S): Milhaud, Phillips, Luening, Ussachevsky, Partch, Cage
COMPOSITIONAL MEDIA: chamber music, ballet, opera, jazz
ITEMS OF INTEREST: teacher — University of Illinois; compositions incorporate serial, aleatory, microtonal, other nonstandard tuning

Jones, Daniel

BIRTH: December 7, 1912 — Pembroke, Wales
TEACHER(S): Sir Henry Wood, Farjeon
COMPOSITIONAL MEDIA: orchestra, chamber music, keyboard, choral, opera, songs, theatrical, books
ITEMS OF INTEREST: held Mendelssohn Traveling Scholarship for 5 years

Jones, Quincy

BIRTH: March 14, 1933 — Chicago, IL
TEACHER(S): Boulanger, Messiaen
COMPOSITIONAL MEDIA: songs, popular, jazz, film and/or T.V.
ITEMS OF INTEREST: professional jazz trumpeter, composer, conductor, record producer since the '70s; best known works include jazz arrangements of movie scores and record production of contemporary rock performers

Joplin, Scott

BIRTH: November 24, 1868 — Texarkana, TX
DEATH: April 1, 1917 — New York, NY
COMPOSITIONAL MEDIA: keyboard, popular, jazz
ITEMS OF INTEREST: best known works include ragtime songs — "The Entertainer," "Maple Leaf Rag"

Josquin des Prez — see des Pres, Josquin

K

Kabalevsky, Dmitri Borisovich (kah bah lev' skē)

BIRTH: December 30, 1904 — St. Petersburg, Russia
DEATH: February 18, 1987
TEACHER(S): Miaskovsky
COMPOSITIONAL MEDIA: orchestra, chamber music, keyboard,
choral, opera, songs, theatrical, film
ITEMS OF INTEREST: teacher — Moscow Conservatory

Kagel, Mauricio

BIRTH: December 24, 1931 — Buenos Aires, Argentina
COMPOSITIONAL MEDIA: chamber music, keyboard, electronic,
theatrical, film
ITEMS OF INTEREST: director — Institute for New Music, Cologne;
compositions incorporate aleatory, audio-visual, electronic, tape,
techniques

Kay, Ulysses

BIRTH: January 7, 1917 — Tucson, AR
TEACHER(S): Hanson, Bernard Rogers, Hindemith, Luening
COMPOSITIONAL MEDIA: orchestra, chamber music, ballet,
keyboard, choral, opera, songs, theatrical
ITEMS OF INTEREST: teacher — City University of New York

Kennan, Kent

BIRTH: April 18, 1913 — Milwaukee, WI
TEACHER(S): Pizzetti, H. Johnson, Hanson, Bernard Rogers
COMPOSITIONAL MEDIA: orchestra, chamber music, keyboard,
choral, songs, books
ITEMS OF INTEREST: teacher — University of Texas at Austin,
pedagogical texts are used in numerous college music courses

Kern, Jerome

BIRTH: January 27, 1885 — New York, NY
DEATH: November 11, 1945 — New York, NY
TEACHER(S): his mother, Gallico, Lambert, Pearce, von Doenhoff
COMPOSITIONAL MEDIA: songs, theatrical, popular
ITEMS OF INTEREST: best known works include Broadway show
"Showboat"

Khachaturian, Aram Ilich (hah tcha tu ryan')

BIRTH: June 6, 1903 — Tiflis, Russia
DEATH: May 1, 1978 — Moscow, Russia
TEACHER(S): Gnessin, Miaskovsky
COMPOSITIONAL MEDIA: orchestra, chamber music, ballet,
keyboard, choral, theatrical, film
ITEMS OF INTEREST: teacher — Moscow Conservatory, Gnessin
Institute; compositions incorporated folk materials; best known works
include "Sabre Dance" which is contained in the ballet "Gayane"

Kirchner, Leon

BIRTH: January 24, 1919 — Brooklyn, NY
TEACHER(S): Stravinsky, Bloch, Sessions, Schoenberg, Toch
COMPOSITIONAL MEDIA: chamber music, keyboard, choral,
opera, electronic
ITEMS OF INTEREST: teacher — Mills College, Harvard University;
Pulitzer Prize winner

Klosé, Hyacinthe-Eléonore

BIRTH: October 11, 1808 — Isle of Corfu, Greece
DEATH: August 29, 1880 — Paris, France
COMPOSITIONAL MEDIA: books
ITEMS OF INTEREST: teacher — Paris Conservatory; best known
works include pedagogical materials for the clarinet

Kodály, Zoltán (koh′ dah ē)

BIRTH: December 16, 1882 — Kecskemét, Hungary
DEATH: March 6, 1967 — Budapest, Hungary
TEACHER(S): Koessler
COMPOSITIONAL MEDIA. orchestra, chamber music, keyboard,
choral, opera, songs, books
ITEMS OF INTEREST. collaborated with Bartok collecting folksongs;
his concepts of music education for young people are widely used
throughout the world today

Köhler, Louis

BIRTH: September 5, 1820 — Brunswick, Germany
DEATH: February 16, 1886 — Königsberg, Germany
TEACHER(S): Sechter, Seyfried
COMPOSITIONAL MEDIA: orchestra, ballet, choral, opera, books
ITEMS OF INTEREST: established piano school, published piano
methods and materials which are still used today

Korngold, Erich Wolfgang

BIRTH: May 29, 1897 — Brno, Austria
DEATH: November 29, 1957 — Hollywood, CA
TEACHER(S): R. Fuchs, Zemlinsky, Gradener
COMPOSITIONAL MEDIA: orchestra, chamber music, keyboard,
opera, songs, theatrical, film
ITEMS OF INTEREST: settled in U.S., 1934; composed for Warner
Brothers' films

Kraft, William

BIRTH: September 6, 1923 — Chicago, IL
TEACHER(S): Luening, Lockwood, Beeson, Cowell, Ussachevsky
COMPOSITIONAL MEDIA: orchestra, chamber music, choral,
theatrical, film, T.V.

ITEMS OF INTEREST: former tympanist Los Angeles Philharmonic, conductor of chamber music ensembles and various new music series

Krebs, Johann Ludwig

BIRTH: October 10, 1713 — Buttelstädt, Germany
DEATH: January 4, 1780 — Altenburg, Germany
TEACHER(S): his father, J.S. Bach
COMPOSITIONAL MEDIA: chamber music, keyboard, choral
ITEMS OF INTEREST: Bach's assistant at Collegium Musicum

Krebs, Carl August

BIRTH: January 16, 1804 — Nuremberg, Germany
DEATH: May 16, 1880 — Dresden, Germany
TEACHER(S): Seyfried
COMPOSITIONAL MEDIA: keyboard, choral, opera, songs
ITEMS OF INTEREST: director — Hamburg Opera, Kapellmeister — Dresden court

Kreisler, Fritz

BIRTH: February 2, 1875 — Vienna, Austria
DEATH: January 29, 1962 — New York, NY
TEACHER(S): Delibes, Bruckner
COMPOSITIONAL MEDIA: chamber music, operettas
ITEMS OF INTEREST: settled in New York, 1940; virtuoso violin performer; composed many violin pieces some of which at first he attributed to other composers

Krenek, Ernst

BIRTH: August 23, 1900—Vienna, Austria   DEATH: Dec. 22, 1991
TEACHER(S): Schreker
COMPOSITIONAL MEDIA: orchestra, chamber music, ballet, keyboard, choral, opera, electronic, theatrical, books

ITEMS OF INTEREST: settled in U.S., 1938; compositions incorporate serial and electronic techniques

Krieger, Johann

BIRTH: December 28, 1651 — Nuremberg, Germany
DEATH: July 18, 1735 — Zittau, Germany
TEACHER(S): J. Philipp Krieger (his brother)
COMPOSITIONAL MEDIA: keyboard, choral
ITEMS OF INTEREST: succeeded his brother as court organist at Bayreuth

Krieger, Johann Philipp

BIRTH: February 25, 1649 — Nuremberg, Germany
DEATH: February 7, 1725 — Weissenfels, Germany
TEACHER(S): Drechsel, Schütz, Schröder
COMPOSITIONAL MEDIA: chamber music, keyboard, choral, opera
ITEMS OF INTEREST: court organist at Beyreuth

Kubik, Gail

BIRTH: Sept. 5, 1914 — S. Coffeyville, OK   DEATH: July 20, 1984
TEACHER(S): Bernard Rogers, Sowerby, Piston, N. Boulanger
COMPOSITIONAL MEDIA: orchestra, chamber music, ballet, keyboard, choral, opera, songs, film, T.V.
ITEMS OF INTEREST: teacher — several U.S. universities, Pulitzer Prize winner

Kuhlau, Friedrick

BIRTH: September 11, 1786 — Ulzen, Germany
DEATH: March 12, 1832 — Copenhagen, Denmark
TEACHER(S): Schwenke
COMPOSITIONAL MEDIA: chamber music, keyboard, choral, songs, theatrical
ITEMS OF INTEREST: best known works include instructive piano pieces

Kuhnau, Johann

BIRTH: April 6, 1660 — Geising, Saxony
DEATH: June 5, 1722 — Leipzig, Germany
TEACHER(S): Hering, Albrici, Edelmann
COMPOSITIONAL MEDIA: harpsichord, choral
ITEMS OF INTEREST: musical director of University of Leipzig

Kurka, Robert

BIRTH: December 22, 1921 — Cicero, IL
DEATH: December 12, 1957 — New York, NY
TEACHER(S): Luening, Milhaud
COMPOSITIONAL MEDIA: orchestra, chamber music, keyboard, choral, opera
ITEMS OF INTEREST: teacher — City College of New York, Queens College

L

Laderman, Ezra

BIRTH: June 29, 1924 — Brooklyn, NY
TEACHER(S): Luening, Moore, Wolpe
COMPOSITIONAL MEDIA: orchestra, chamber music, keyboard, opera, songs, theatrical, film, T.V.
ITEMS OF INTEREST: teacher — Sarah Lawrence College, State University of New York at Binghamton

Lalo, Édouard

BIRTH: January 27, 1823 — Lille, France
DEATH: April 22, 1892 — Paris, France
TEACHER(S): Baumann, Schulhoff, Crèvecoeur
COMPOSITIONAL MEDIA: orchestra, chamber music, ballet, keyboard, choral, opera, songs
ITEMS OF INTEREST: marriage to Mlle. Bernier de Maligny rekindled his career

Langlais, Jean

BIRTH: February 15, 1907 — La Fontenelle   DEATH: May 8, 1991
TEACHER(S): Dupre, Dukas
COMPOSITIONAL MEDIA: orchestra, organ, choral, songs
ITEMS OF INTEREST: organist, blind from childhood

Lassus, Orlando di

BIRTH: 1532 — Mons
DEATH: June 14, 1594 — Munich, Germany
COMPOSITIONAL MEDIA: chamber music, choral
ITEMS OF INTEREST: composed hundreds of vocal pieces, best known works include his Italian madrigals and French chansons

Legrand, Michel

BIRTH: February 24, 1932 — Paris, France
COMPOSITIONAL MEDIA: songs, theatrical, popular, jazz, film and/or T.V.
ITEMS OF INTEREST: professional jazz pianist, best known works include the film score "The Umbrellas of Cherbourg"

Lehár, Franz (lä' hahr)

BIRTH: April 30, 1870 — Komorn, Hungary
DEATH: October 24, 1948 — Bad Ischl, Austria
TEACHER(S): Foerster, Fibich

COMPOSITIONAL MEDIA: orchestra, keyboard, operettas, songs, theatrical, popular, film, concert band marches

ITEMS OF INTEREST: best known works include the operetta "The Merry Widow"

Lennon, John

BIRTH: October 9, 1940 — Liverpool, England
DEATH: December 8, 1980 — New York, NY
COMPOSITIONAL MEDIA: songs, rock, film and/or T.V.
ITEMS OF INTEREST: one of the most important song writers of the rock era; his collaboration with Paul McCartney changed the sound and meaning of music from the 1960's on; best known works include "Eleanor Rigby," "Yesterday," "A Hard Day's Night"

Leoncavallo, Ruggiero

BIRTH: April 23, 1857 — Naples
DEATH: August 9, 1919 — Montecatini
TEACHER(S): B. Cesi, M. Ruta, L. Rossi
COMPOSITIONAL MEDIA: orchestra, ballet, keyboard, operettas, songs
ITEMS OF INTEREST: best known works include his opera "I Pagliacci"

Levant, Oscar

BIRTH: December 27, 1906 — Pittsburgh, PA
DEATH: August 14, 1972 — Beverly Hills, CA
TEACHER(S): Stojowski, Schoenberg, Schillinger
COMPOSITIONAL MEDIA: orchestra, chamber music, keyboard, film and/or T.V., books
ITEMS OF INTEREST: professional pianist; radio and T.V. personality

Lewis, John

BIRTH: May 3, 1920 — La Grange, IL
COMPOSITIONAL MEDIA: songs, jazz, film and/or T.V.
ITEMS OF INTEREST: Musical Director of the Modern Jazz Quartet which blended elements of classical music with jazz, best known works include "Django" and the score to the movie "No Sun in Venice"

Liszt, Franz

BIRTH: October 22, 1811 — Raiding, Hungary
DEATH: July 31, 1886 — Bayreuth, Germany
TEACHER(S): Czerny, Salieri, Reicha, Paer
COMPOSITIONAL MEDIA: orchestra, chamber music, keyboard, choral, opera, songs, books
ITEMS OF INTEREST: professional pianist who is best known works include his piano compositions and pedagogical books

Loesser, Frank

BIRTH: June 29, 1910 — New York, NY
DEATH: July 28, 1969 — New York, NY
COMPOSITIONAL MEDIA: songs, theatrical, popular
ITEMS OF INTEREST: best known works include Broadway musicals — "Guys and Dolls," "The Most Happy Fella," as well as numerous standard songs

Loewe, Frederick

BIRTH: June 10, 1901 — Vienna   DEATH: February 14, 1988
TEACHER(S): Busoni, d'Albert, Reznicek
COMPOSITIONAL MEDIA: songs, theatrical, popular
ITEMS OF INTEREST: best known works include Broadway musicals — "Brigadoon," "My Fair Lady"

Luening, Otto

BIRTH: June 15, 1900 — Milwaukee, WI
TEACHER(S): Jarnach, Busoni
COMPOSITIONAL MEDIA: orchestra, chamber music, ballet,
keyboard, choral, opera, songs, electronic, theatrical
ITEMS OF INTEREST: teachers — various colleges, co-director
Princeton-Columbia Electronic Music Center; compositions incor-
porate tape and electronic techniques

Lully, Jean-Baptiste

BIRTH: November 28, 1632 — Florence, Italy
DEATH: March 22, 1687 — Paris, France
TEACHER(S): Roberday, Gigault
COMPOSITIONAL MEDIA: chamber music, ballet, choral, opera,
songs, theatrical
ITEMS OF INTEREST: composer — King Louis XIV

Lutoslawski, Witold

BIRTH: Jan. 25, 1913 — Warsaw, Poland DEATH: Feb. 7, 1994
COMPOSITIONAL MEDIA: orchestra, chamber music, keyboard,
choral, songs, theatrical, film and/or radio
ITEMS OF INTEREST: compositions incorporate serial and aleatoric
techniques and folk music

M

MacDowell, Edward Alexander

BIRTH: December 18, 1860 — New York, NY
DEATH: January 23, 1908 — New York, NY
TEACHER(S): Raff
COMPOSITIONAL MEDIA: orchestra, keyboard, choral, songs
ITEMS OF INTEREST: teacher — Columbia University, best known
works include "To a Wild Rose" in "Woodland Sketches"

Machaut, Guillaume de (măh shōh′)

BIRTH: 1300 — Machaut, Champagne, France
DEATH: April 1377 — Rheims, France
COMPOSITIONAL MEDIA: choral
ITEMS OF INTEREST: at the court of Charles V of France

Mahler, Gustav

BIRTH: July 7, 1860 — Kalischt, Bohemia
DEATH: May 18, 1911 — Vienna, Austria
TEACHER(S): R. Fuchs
COMPOSITIONAL MEDIA: orchestra, keyboard, choral, songs
ITEMS OF INTEREST: conducted numerous orchestras in Europe
and U.S., compositions used large resources of performers

Mancini, Henry

BIRTH: April 16, 1924   DEATH: June 14, 1994
TEACHER(S): his father, Tedsco, Krenek, Sendry
COMPOSITIONAL MEDIA: songs, popular, jazz, film and/or T.V.
ITEMS OF INTEREST: best known works include film scores —
"Breakfast at Tiffany's", reached national prominence with TV score
"Peter Gunn"

Marchand, Louis (mahr shan')

BIRTH: February 2, 1669 — Lyon, France
DEATH: February 17, 1732 — Paris, France
COMPOSITIONAL MEDIA: keyboard, choral, opera
ITEMS OF INTEREST: organist of the royal chapel in Paris

Markevich, Igor (mǎhr kěh' vich)

BIRTH: July 27, 1912 — Kiev, Russia   DEATH: March 7, 1983
TEACHER(S): N. Boulanger, Rieti
COMPOSITIONAL MEDIA: orchestra, chamber music, ballet,
keyboard, choral
ITEMS OF INTEREST: career emphasis changed from composing to
conducting

Martin, Frank

BIRTH: September 15, 1890 — Geneva, Switzerland
DEATH: November 21, 1974 — Naarden, the Netherlands
TEACHER(S): Lauber
COMPOSITIONAL MEDIA: orchestra, chamber music, ballet,
keyboard, choral, opera, songs, theatrical
ITEMS OF INTEREST: teacher — Dalcroze Institute, Cologne,
Hochschule fur Musik;
compositions incorporate twelve-tone techniques and folk song
materials

Mascagni, Pietro (mas kahn' yē)

BIRTH: December 7, 1863 — Livorno, Italy
DEATH: August 2, 1945 — Rome, Italy
TEACHER(S): A. Soffredini, Ponchielli
COMPOSITIONAL MEDIA: orchestra, chamber music, choral,
opera, songs
ITEMS OF INTEREST: best known works include the opera
"Cavalleria Rusticana"

Mason, Lowell

BIRTH: January 8, 1792 — Medfield, MA
DEATH: August 11, 1872 — Orange, NJ
COMPOSITIONAL MEDIA: songs, books
ITEMS OF INTEREST: a strong force in the early development of music education in the U.S.

Massenet, Jules (mahss nā')

BIRTH: May 12, 1842 — Montaud, France
DEATH: August 13, 1912 — Paris, France
TEACHER(S): Reber, Ambroise Thomas
COMPOSITIONAL MEDIA: orchestra, chamber music, ballet, keyboard, choral, opera, songs, theatrical
ITEMS OF INTEREST: teacher — Paris Conservatory; pupils included G. Charpentier, Koechlin, Leroux, Enescu; best known works include the opera "Manon"

Mayuzumi, Toshirō

BIRTH: February 20, 1929 — Yokohama, Japan
TEACHER(S): Ikenouchi, T. Aubin
COMPOSITIONAL MEDIA: orchestra, chamber music, ballet, choral, opera, electronic, film
ITEMS OF INTEREST: compositions incorporate works on tape

McCartney, Paul

BIRTH: June 18, 1942 — Liverpool, England
COMPOSITIONAL MEDIA: songs, rock, film and/or T.V.
ITEMS OF INTEREST: one of the most important song writers of the rock era; his collaboration with John Lennon changed the sound and meaning of music from the 1960's on; best known works include "Eleanor Rigby," "Yesterday," "A Hard Day's Night;" since the break up of the Beatles in the 1970's, he has continued a successful composing and performing career

McDowell, John Herbert

BIRTH: December 21, 1926 — Washington, DC
TEACHER(S): Luening, Beeson, Goeb
COMPOSITIONAL MEDIA: orchestra, chamber music, ballet, choral, opera, electronic, theatrical, film, T.V.
ITEMS OF INTEREST: compositions incorporate mixed media

McKuen, Rod Marvin

BIRTH: April 29, 1933 — Oakland, CA
TEACHER(S): Stravinsky, Mancini, Greenslade
COMPOSITIONAL MEDIA: orchestra, ballet, opera, songs, popular
ITEMS OF INTEREST: best known works include songs — "If You Go Away," "Jean"

Mendelssohn, Felix

BIRTH: February 3, 1809 — Hamburg, Germany
DEATH: November 4, 1847 — Leipzig, Germany
TEACHER(S): Zelter, Moscheles
COMPOSITIONAL MEDIA: orchestra, chamber music, keyboard, choral, opera, songs, theatrical
ITEMS OF INTEREST: large output of music — best known works include incidental music to Shakespeare's "A Midsummer Night's Dream", the oratorio "Elijah", and his symphonies

Mennin, Peter

BIRTH: May 17, 1923 — Erie, PA
DEATH: June 17, 1983 — New York, NY
TEACHER(S): Lockwood, Bernard Rogers, Hanson
COMPOSITIONAL MEDIA: orchestra, chamber music, keyboard, choral, songs
ITEMS OF INTEREST: director — Peabody Conservatory, president — Juilliard School

Menotti, Gian Carlo

BIRTH: July 7, 1911 — Cadegliano, Italy
TEACHER(S): Scalero
COMPOSITIONAL MEDIA: orchestra, ballet, keyboard, opera, songs, film, radio
ITEMS OF INTEREST: teacher — Curtis Institute, Philadelphia; Pulitzer Prize winner; best known works include opera "Amahl and the Night Visitors"

Messiaen, Olivier (mĕh sē yän')

BIRTH: December 10, 1908 — Avignon   DEATH: April 28, 1992
TEACHER(S): J. and N. Gallon, G. Caussade, Emmanuel, Dupre, Dukas
COMPOSITIONAL MEDIA: orchestra, chamber music, keyboard, songs
ITEMS OF INTEREST: teacher — Paris Conservatory; pupils included Boulez, Barraque, Amy, Henry, Stockhausen, Xenakis; compositions incorporate extra musical sources, chants, Oriental elements

Meyerbeer, Giacomo

BIRTH: September 5, 1791 — Berlin, Germany
DEATH: May 2, 1864 — Paris, France
TEACHER(S): Clementi, Zelter, Abbe Vogler
COMPOSITIONAL MEDIA: chamber music, choral, opera, songs, theatrical
ITEMS OF INTEREST: best known works include opera "Les Huguenots"

Milhaud, Darius (mē yōh')

BIRTH: September 4, 1892 — Aix-en-Provence, France
DEATH: June 22, 1974 — Geneva, Switzerland
TEACHER(S): Leroux, Gedalge, Widor, d'Indy

COMPOSITIONAL MEDIA: orchestra, chamber music, ballet, keyboard, choral, opera, songs, theatrical, film
ITEMS OF INTEREST: compositions incorporate polytonal techniques

Mingus, Charles

BIRTH: April 22, 1922 — Nogales, AZ
DEATH: January 8, 1979 — Cuernavaca, Mexico
COMPOSITIONAL MEDIA: songs, jazz, film and T.V.
ITEMS OF INTEREST: professional jazz bassist; best known works include "Pithecanthropus Erectus," "Goodbye Pork Pie Hat"

Monk, Thelonious

BIRTH: October 10, 1918 — Rock Mountain, NC
DEATH: February 17, 1982 — Weehawken, New Jersey
COMPOSITIONAL MEDIA: songs, jazz
ITEMS OF INTEREST: professional jazz pianist, best known works include "Blue Monk," "'Round Midnight"

Monteverdi, Claudio

BIRTH: May 15, 1567 — Cremona
DEATH: November 29, 1643 — Venice
TEACHER(S): Ingegneri
COMPOSITIONAL MEDIA: ballet, choral, opera, songs
ITEMS OF INTEREST: director of music — San Marco, Venice; best known works include the "Lament" from the opera "L'Arianna," and for his operas "Orfeo," "L'Incaronazione di Poppea"

Moore, Douglas

BIRTH: August 10, 1893 — Cutchogue, NY
DEATH: July 25, 1969 — Greenport, NY
TEACHER(S): Parker, d'Indy, N. Boulanger, Bloch
COMPOSITIONAL MEDIA: orchestra, chamber music, choral, opera, songs

ITEMS OF INTEREST: teacher — Columbia University, Pulitzer Prize winner, best known works include opera "Ballad of Baby Doe"

Morley, Thomas

BIRTH: 1557
DEATH: October 1602
TEACHER(S): Byrd
COMPOSITIONAL MEDIA: choral, books
ITEMS OF INTEREST: best known works include his madrigals, lute music

Mozart, Leopold (moh′ tsahrt)

BIRTH: November 14, 1719 — Augsburg, Austria
DEATH: May 28, 1787 — Salzburg, Austria
COMPOSITIONAL MEDIA: chamber music, keyboard, choral, opera, songs, books
ITEMS OF INTEREST: father of W.A. Mozart

Mozart, Wolfgang Amadeus (moh′ tsahrt)

BIRTH: January 27, 1756 — Salzburg, Austria
DEATH: December 5, 1791 — Vienna, Austria
TEACHER(S): Leopold Mozart (his father), Padre Martini
COMPOSITIONAL MEDIA: orchestra, chamber music, keyboard, choral, opera, songs
ITEMS OF INTEREST: the most important composer of the late 1700's; child prodigy — first public performance at 6; very prolific — in his short life of 35 years, he composed over 600 works; much of his music (including operas, symphonies, string quartets, keyboard music) is widely performed today

Mulligan, Gerry

BIRTH: April 6, 1927 — New York, NY

COMPOSITIONAL MEDIA: jazz, film and/or T.V.

ITEMS OF INTEREST: professional baritone saxophonist; best known works include jazz compositions — "Utter Chaos," "Walking Shoes"

Mussorgsky, Modest Petrovich

BIRTH: March 21, 1839 — Karevo, Russia

DEATH: March 28, 1881 — St. Petersburg, Russia

COMPOSITIONAL MEDIA: orchestra, keyboard, choral, opera, songs

ITEMS OF INTEREST: best known works include opera "Boris Godunov," orchestra composition "Night on Bald Mountain," piano piece "Pictures at an Exhibition" which is most popular in its orchestral version

N

Nabokov, Nicolas (näh bŏ′ kŏv)

BIRTH: April 17, 1903 — Lubcha, Russia

DEATH: April 6, 1978 — New York, NY

TEACHER(S): Rebikov, Busoni, Juon

COMPOSITIONAL MEDIA: orchestra, chamber music, ballet, keyboard, choral, opera, songs

ITEMS OF INTEREST: settled in U.S., 1933; teacher — various schools including Peabody Conservatory, State University of New York at Buffalo, New York University

Nelhybel, Vaclav

BIRTH: September 24, 1919 — Polanka, Czechoslovakia
COMPOSITIONAL MEDIA: orchestra, chamber music, ballet, keyboard, choral, opera, concert band
ITEMS OF INTEREST: music director of Radio Free Europe in Munich, 1950-57; settled in the U.S., 1957; very active as composer for school performing groups

Nelson, Ron J.

BIRTH: December 14, 1929 — Joliet, IL
TEACHER(S): Hanson, Bernard Rogers, L. Mennini, Barlow, Honegger, T. Aubin
COMPOSITIONAL MEDIA: orchestra, choral, opera
ITEMS OF INTEREST: teacher — Brown University

Nicolai, Otto

BIRTH: June 9, 1810 — Königsberg, Germany
DEATH: May 11, 1849 — Berlin, Germany
TEACHER(S): Zelter
COMPOSITIONAL MEDIA: orchestra, chamber music, keyboard, choral, opera, songs
ITEMS OF INTEREST: best known works include opera "The Merry Wives of Windsor"

Nielsen, Carl

BIRTH: June 9, 1865 — Norre-Lyndelse, Denmark
DEATH: October 3, 1931 — Copenhagen, Denmark
TEACHER(S): Gade
COMPOSITIONAL MEDIA: orchestra, chamber music, keyboard, choral, opera, songs, theatrical
ITEMS OF INTEREST: professional violinist; conductor — Copenhagen Opera, Copenhagen Musical Society

Nilsson, Bo

BIRTH: May 1, 1937 — Skelleftea, Sweden
COMPOSITIONAL MEDIA: orchestra, chamber music, keyboard, electronic
ITEMS OF INTEREST: compositions incorporate electronic, serial techniques

Nono, Luigi

BIRTH: January 29, 1924 — Venice, Italy   DEATH: May 8, 1990
TEACHER(S): Malipiero, Maderna
COMPOSITIONAL MEDIA: orchestra, chamber music, ballet, keyboard, choral, opera, songs, electronic
ITEMS OF INTEREST: compositions incorporate electronic, taped, serial techniques

Nordoff, Paul

BIRTH: June 4, 1909 — Philadelphia, PA
DEATH: January 18, 1977 — Herdecke, Germany
TEACHER(S): R. Goldmark
COMPOSITIONAL MEDIA: orchestra, chamber music, ballet, opera, songs
ITEMS OF INTEREST: very active in the field of music therapy

O

Obrecht, Jacob

BIRTH: November 22, 1450 — Netherlands
DEATH: 1505 — Ferrara, Italy
COMPOSITIONAL MEDIA: choral
ITEMS OF INTEREST: music director — Notre Dame, Antwerp

Offenbach, Jacques

BIRTH: June 20, 1819 — Cologne, Germany
DEATH: October 5, 1880 — Paris, France
TEACHER(S): Halevy
COMPOSITIONAL MEDIA: opera, operettas
ITEMS OF INTEREST: settled in Paris; best known works include opera "The Tales of Hoffmann", operetta "La vie parisienne"

Orff, Carl

BIRTH: July 10, 1895 — Munich
DEATH: March 29, 1982 — New York, NY
TEACHER(S): Kaminski
COMPOSITIONAL MEDIA: orchestra, choral, opera, books
ITEMS OF INTEREST: best known works include oratorio "Carmina burana"; active in music education using xylophones, percussion instruments, movement as the basis of early learning

Ornstein, Leo

BIRTH: December 11, 1895 — Kremenchug, Russia
TEACHER(S): his father, Pachalski, Tapper, Goetschius
COMPOSITIONAL MEDIA: orchestra, chamber music, keyboard, choral, songs
ITEMS OF INTEREST: professional pianist whose concerts often included his own and other contemporary piano compositions

Overton, Hall

BIRTH: February 23, 1920 — Bangor, MI
DEATH: November 24, 1972 — New York, NY
TEACHER(S): Persichetti, Riegger, Milhaud
COMPOSITIONAL MEDIA: orchestra, chamber music, ballet, keyboard, opera, songs
ITEMS OF INTEREST: teacher — New School for Social Research, Juilliard School; jazz pianist

P

Pachelbel, Johann

BIRTH: September 1, 1653 — Nuremberg
DEATH: March 3, 1706 — Nuremberg
COMPOSITIONAL MEDIA: organ, harpsichord
ITEMS OF INTEREST: organist at various churches including
Eisenach

Paderewski, Ignace Jan (pah děh rev' skē)

BIRTH: November 18, 1860 — Kurylowka, Russia
DEATH: June 29, 1941 — New York, NY
TEACHER(S): Leschetizky
COMPOSITIONAL MEDIA: orchestra, keyboard, opera, songs
ITEMS OF INTEREST: professional pianist, held posts in Polish
government

Paganini, Niccolò

BIRTH: October 27, 1782 — Genoa, Italy
DEATH: May 27, 1840 — Nice, France
TEACHER(S): G. Servetto, Costa, Ghiretti, Rolla
COMPOSITIONAL MEDIA: violin music, chamber music
ITEMS OF INTEREST: violin virtuoso, best known works include
violin solos "24 Capricci"

Palestrina, Giovanni Pierluigi da

BIRTH: 1525 — Palestrina, Italy
DEATH: February 2, 1594 — Rome, Italy
TEACHER(S): Le Bel
COMPOSITIONAL MEDIA: choral, songs
ITEMS OF INTEREST: choir master at St. Peter's, Rome; best known works include masses, motets

Parker, Horatio

BIRTH: September 15, 1863 — Auburndale, MA
DEATH: December 18, 1919 — Cedarhurst, NY
TEACHER(S): Chadwick, Rheinberger
COMPOSITIONAL MEDIA: orchestra, chamber music, keyboard, choral, opera, songs
ITEMS OF INTEREST: teacher — Yale; founded and conducted the New Haven Symphony Orchestra, New Haven, CT

Partch, Harry

BIRTH: June 24, 1901 — Oakland, CA
DEATH: September 3, 1974 — San Diego, CA
COMPOSITIONAL MEDIA: chamber music, theatrical
ITEMS OF INTEREST: invented numerous musical instruments, some of which employed a scale consisting of 43 tones to the octave

Peeters, Flor

BIRTH: July 4, 1903 — Thielen, Belgium   DEATH: July 4, 1986
TEACHER(S): Mortelmans
COMPOSITIONAL MEDIA: keyboard, choral, songs, books
ITEMS OF INTEREST: teacher — Lemmens Institute in Malines, Royal Conservatory in Antwerp; professional organist; best known works include his organ compositions, research, pedagogical material

Penderecki, Krzysztof (pĕn dĕh rĕts' kē)

BIRTH: November 23, 1933 — Debica, Poland
COMPOSITIONAL MEDIA: orchestra, chamber music, choral,
opera, songs
ITEMS OF INTEREST: teacher — Music Academy in Cracow, Yale
School of Music; compositions incorporate serial techniques, use of
instruments in unusual ways

Pepusch, Johann Christoph (pā' pŏosh)

BIRTH: 1667 — Berlin, Germany
DEATH: July 20, 1752 — London, England
TEACHER(S): Klingenberg, Grosse
COMPOSITIONAL MEDIA: chamber music, choral, books
ITEMS OF INTEREST: best known works include arranging the
music for opera "The Beggar's Opera"

Pergolesi, Giovanni Battista (per goh lā' zē)

BIRTH: January 4, 1710 — Jesi, Italy
DEATH: March 16, 1736 — Pozzuoli, Italy
TEACHER(S): Durante, Feo
COMPOSITIONAL MEDIA: chamber music, harpsichord,
choral, opera
ITEMS OF INTEREST: choir master to Prince of Stigliano, Naples

Peri, Jacopo

BIRTH: August 20, 1561 — Rome, Italy
DEATH: August 12, 1633 — Florence, Italy
TEACHER(S): Malvezzi
COMPOSITIONAL MEDIA: ballet, choral, opera, songs
ITEMS OF INTEREST: best known works include the first operas —
"Dafne" (1597), "Euridice" (1600)

Perle, George

BIRTH: May 6, 1915 — Bayonne, NJ
TEACHER(S): W. La Violette, Krenek
COMPOSITIONAL MEDIA: orchestra, chamber music, keyboard,
choral, books
ITEMS OF INTEREST: teacher — University of Louisville, University
of California/Davis, Queens College, New York; compositions incorporate twelve-tone techniques

Persichetti, Vincent

BIRTH: June 6, 1915 — Philadelphia, PA   DEATH: Aug. 13, 1987
TEACHER(S): Nordoff, Harris, Reiner
COMPOSITIONAL MEDIA: orchestra, chamber music, keyboard,
choral, songs, concert band, books
ITEMS OF INTEREST: teacher — Philadelphia Conservatory,
Juilliard School

Pezel, Johann Christoph

BIRTH: 1639 — Calau, Germany
DEATH: October 13, 1694 — Bautzen, Germany
COMPOSITIONAL MEDIA: chamber music, choral
ITEMS OF INTEREST: best known works include his music for brass
instruments

Phillips, Burrill

BIRTH: November 9, 1907 — Omaha, NE   DEATH: June 22, 1988
TEACHER(S): Stringham, Bernard Rogers, Hanson
COMPOSITIONAL MEDIA: orchestra, chamber music, ballet,
keyboard, choral, opera, songs, film
ITEMS OF INTEREST: teacher — Eastman School, University of Illinois

Pinkham, Daniel

BIRTH: June 5, 1923 — Lynn, MA

TEACHER(S): Piston, Copland, Barber, Honegger, N. Boulanger
COMPOSITIONAL MEDIA: orchestra, chamber music, keyboard, choral, opera, electronic
ITEMS OF INTEREST: teacher — New England Conservatory, compositions incorporate tape and electronic techniques

Piston, Walter

BIRTH: January 20, 1894 — Rockland, ME
DEATH: November 12, 1976 — Belmont, MA
TEACHER(S): N. Boulanger, Dukas
COMPOSITIONAL MEDIA: orchestra, chamber music, ballet, keyboard, choral, books
ITEMS OF INTEREST: teacher — Harvard University; pupils included Adler, Berger, Bernstein, Carter, Fine, Layton, Shapero, R. Ward; Pulitzer Prize winner

Porter, Cole

BIRTH: June 9, 1891 — Peru, IN
DEATH: October 15, 1964 — Santa Monica, CA
COMPOSITIONAL MEDIA: songs, theatrical, popular
ITEMS OF INTEREST: best known works include Broadway musicals — "Kiss Me Kate," "Silk Stockings;" songs — "Begin the Beguine," "Night and Day"

Porter, Quincy

BIRTH: February 7, 1897 — New Haven, CT
DEATH: November 12, 1966 — Bethany, CT
TEACHER(S): Parker, D.S. Smith, d'Indy, Bloch
COMPOSITIONAL MEDIA: orchestra, chamber music, keyboard, songs
ITEMS OF INTEREST: teacher — Cleveland Institute, Vassar College, New England Conservatory, Yale University; Pulitzer Prize winner

Poulenc, Francis (pōō lank')

BIRTH: January 7, 1899 — Paris, France
DEATH: January 30, 1963 — Paris, France
TEACHER(S): Koechlin
COMPOSITIONAL MEDIA: orchestra, chamber music, ballet, keyboard, choral, opera, songs, theatrical, film
ITEMS OF INTEREST: pianist who accompanied many famous singers of the day; best known works include operas and sacred choral work "Gloria"

Powell, Mel

BIRTH: February 12, 1923 — New York, NY
TEACHER(S): B. Wagenaar, Schillinger, Toch, Hindemith
COMPOSITIONAL MEDIA: orchestra, chamber music, keyboard, electronic
ITEMS OF INTEREST: professional jazz pianist; teacher — Yale University, California Institute of the Arts; compositions incorporate tape and electronic techniques

Praetorius, Michael

BIRTH: February 15, 1571 — Kreuzberg, Germany
DEATH: February 15, 1621 — Wolfenbuttel, Germany
TEACHER(S): G. Gabrieli
COMPOSITIONAL MEDIA: chamber music, choral, books
ITEMS OF INTEREST: wrote over 1,000 sacred choral works

Prokofiev, Sergey Sergeyevitch (prŏh kōh' fyĕf)

BIRTH: April 23, 1891 — Sontzovka, Russia
DEATH: March 5, 1953 — Moscow, Russia
TEACHER(S): Gliere, Rimsky-Korsakov, Whitol, Liadov, Essipova
COMPOSITIONAL MEDIA: orchestra, chamber music, ballet, keyboard, choral, opera
ITEMS OF INTEREST: very prolific in all areas of composition; best

known works include operas — "Love of Three Oranges," "War and Peace;" cantata — "Alexander Nevsky;" ballet — "Romeo and Juliet;" orchestral works — "Classical Symphony," "Suite from Lieutenant Kije"

Puccini, Giacomo (pōōch chē′ nē)

BIRTH: December 22, 1858 — Lucca, Italy
DEATH: November 29, 1924 — Brussels, Belgium
TEACHER(S): Ponchielli
COMPOSITIONAL MEDIA: orchestra, chamber music, organ, choral, opera, songs
ITEMS OF INTEREST: best known works include his operas including "Madama Butterfly", "La Boheme", "Tosca", "Manon Lescaut"

Purcell, Henry (pur′ sĕl)

BIRTH: 1659 — London, England
DEATH: November 21, 1695 — Dean's Yard, Westminster
TEACHER(S): Blow
COMPOSITIONAL MEDIA: orchestra, chamber music, keyboard, choral, opera, songs, theatrical, books
ITEMS OF INTEREST: organist at Westminster Abbey, best known works include opera "Dido and Aeneas"

Q

Quantz, Johann Joachim

BIRTH: January 30, 1697 — Oberscheden, Germany
DEATH: July 12, 1773 — Potsdam, Germany

TEACHER(S): Zelenka, Fux, Gasparini
COMPOSITIONAL MEDIA: chamber music, choral, books
ITEMS OF INTEREST: professional flutist, composer to and teacher of Frederick the Great, best known works include flute compositions

R

Rachmaninov, Sergei Vassilievich (răh măh′ nē nŏhf)

BIRTH: April 1, 1873 — Oneg, Russia
DEATH: March 28, 1943 — Beverly Hills, CA
TEACHER(S): Taneiev, Arensky
COMPOSITIONAL MEDIA: orchestra, chamber music, keyboard, choral, opera, songs
ITEMS OF INTEREST: professional pianist, settled in U.S. in 1935, best known for his piano concerto

Rameau, Jean-Philippe (răh moh′)

BIRTH: September 25, 1683 — Dijon, France
DEATH: September 12, 1764 Paris, France
COMPOSITIONAL MEDIA: chamber music, ballet, harpsichord, choral, opera, books
ITEMS OF INTEREST: teacher — harpsichord, theory

Raposo, Joseph G.

BIRTH: February 8, 1937 — Fall River, MA
DEATH: February 5, 1989 — Bronxville, NY
TEACHER(S): Boulanger
COMPOSITIONAL MEDIA: Songs, theatrical, popular, film and/or TV
ITEMS OF INTEREST: best known works include children's TV shows — "Sesame Street," "The Electric Company," "The Muppet Show"

Ravel, Maurice (răh vĕl′)

BIRTH: March 7, 1875 — Ciboure, France
DEATH: December 28, 1937 — Paris, France
TEACHER(S): Gédalge, Fauré
COMPOSITIONAL MEDIA: orchestra, chamber music, ballet,
keyboard, choral, opera
ITEMS OF INTEREST: along with Debussy, was the premier com-
poser in the Impressionistic style; best known works include ballet
"Daphnis et Chloe", orchestral work "Bolero", numerous piano
compositions

Read, Gardner

BIRTH: January 2, 1913 — Evanston, IL
TEACHER(S): Bernard Rogers, Hanson, Pizzetti, Sibelius, Copland
COMPOSITIONAL MEDIA: orchestra, chamber music, keyboard,
choral, opera, songs, theatrical, books
ITEMS OF INTEREST: teacher — Boston University, his text on
notation is used as a reference by most young composers/arrangers

Reed, H. Owen

BIRTH: June 17, 1910 — Odessa, MO
TEACHER(S): Bernard Rogers, Hanson, Martinu, Harris
COMPOSITIONAL MEDIA: orchestra, chamber music, ballet,
keyboard, choral, opera, songs, concert band, books
ITEMS OF INTEREST: teacher — Michigan State University

Reger, Max (rā′ gĕr)

BIRTH: March 19, 1873 — Brand, Bavaria
DEATH: May 11, 1916 — Leipzig, Germany
TEACHER(S): H. Riemann
COMPOSITIONAL MEDIA: orchestra, chamber music, keyboard,
choral

ITEMS OF INTEREST: professional pianist; teacher — Wiesbaden Conservatory, Munich Academy, Leipzig Conservatory

Reinecke, Carl

BIRTH: June 23, 1824 — Altona, Germany
DEATH: March 10, 1910 — Leipzig, Germany
TEACHER(S): his father
COMPOSITIONAL MEDIA: orchestra, chamber music, keyboard, choral, songs, books
ITEMS OF INTEREST: professional pianist; teacher — Cologne Conservatory, Leipzig Conservatory; pupils included Grieg; conductor of various orchestras

Respighi, Ottorino (rēh spē' gē)

BIRTH: July 9, 1879 — Bologna, Italy
DEATH: April 18, 1936 — Rome, Italy
TEACHER(S): Martucci, Rimsky-Korsakov, Bruch
COMPOSITIONAL MEDIA: orchestra, chamber music, ballet, keyboard, choral, opera, songs
ITEMS OF INTEREST: teacher — Accademia di Santa Cecilia in Rome; best known works include orchestral works "The Pines of Rome", "The Fountains of Rome"

Reynolds, Roger

BIRTH: July 18, 1934 — Detroit, MI
TEACHER(S): Finney, Gerhard
COMPOSITIONAL MEDIA: orchestra, chamber music, keyboard, choral, electronic
ITEMS OF INTEREST: teacher — University of California, San Diego; compositions incorporate graphic notation and mixed media

Richter, Ernst Friedrich Eduard

BIRTH: October 24, 1808 — Gross-Schonau, Saxony
DEATH: April 9, 1879 — Leipzig, Germany
TEACHER(S): Weinlig
COMPOSITIONAL MEDIA: chamber music, keyboard, choral,
songs, books
ITEMS OF INTEREST: teacher — Leipzig Conservatory

Riegger, Wallingford

BIRTH: April 29, 1885 — Albany, GA
DEATH: April 2, 1961 — New York, NY
TEACHER(S): his father and mother, Goetschius, Schroeder
COMPOSITIONAL MEDIA: orchestra, chamber music, ballet,
keyboard, choral, songs, books
ITEMS OF INTEREST: compositions incorporate twelve-tone
techniques; wrote many pedagogical pieces, often with pseudonyms

Rimsky-Korsakov, Nikolai Andreievich

BIRTH: March 18, 1844 — Tikhvin, Russia
DEATH: June 21, 1908 — Liubensk, Russia
TEACHER(S): Balakirev
COMPOSITIONAL MEDIA: orchestra, chamber music, keyboard,
choral, opera, songs, concert band, books
ITEMS OF INTEREST: teacher — St. Petersburg Conservatory;
pupils included Glazunov, Ippolitov-Ivanov, Miaskovsky, Prokofiev,
Respighi, Steinberg, Stravinsky; best known works include orchestral
suite "Scheherazade", orchestra piece "Capriccio espagnol", his text
on orchestration

Rochberg, George

BIRTH: July 5, 1918 — Paterson, NJ
TEACHER(S): G. Szell, H. Weisse, Scalero, Mennotti
COMPOSITIONAL MEDIA: orchestra, chamber music, keyboard,

choral, songs, concert band, books
ITEMS OF INTEREST: teacher — Curtis Institute, University of
Pennsylvania; compositions incorporate twelve-tone techniques

Rodgers, Richard

BIRTH: June 28, 1902 — New York, NY
DEATH: December 30, 1979 — New York, NY
COMPOSITIONAL MEDIA: songs, theatrical, popular
ITEMS OF INTEREST: best known works include Broadway musicals
— "Oklahoma," "Carousel," "South Pacific" (for which he won a
Pulitzer Prize), "The King and I," "Flower Drum Song"

Rogers, Bernard

BIRTH: February 4, 1893 — New York, NY
DEATH: May 24, 1968 — Rochester, NY
TEACHER(S): Farwell, Bloch, N. Boulanger, Bridge
COMPOSITIONAL MEDIA: orchestra, chamber music, choral,
opera, books
ITEMS OF INTEREST: teacher — Eastman School of Music, pupils
included many well known 20th century American composers

Rorem, Ned

BIRTH: October 23, 1923 — Richmond, IN
TEACHER(S): Sowerby, B. Wagenaar, Copland, Thomson, Honegger
COMPOSITIONAL MEDIA: orchestra, chamber music, keyboard,
choral, opera, songs, books
ITEMS OF INTEREST: teacher — State University of New York at
Buffalo, University of Utah; Pulitzer Prize winner; best known works
include songs and song cycles

Rossini, Gioacchino

BIRTH: February 29, 1792 — Pesaro, Italy
DEATH: November 13, 1868 — Paris, France

TEACHER(S): Tesei, Mattei, Cavedagni
COMPOSITIONAL MEDIA: orchestra, chamber music, keyboard, choral, opera, songs
ITEMS OF INTEREST: best known works include opera "William Tell"

Rousseau, Jean-Jacques

BIRTH: June 28, 1712 — Geneva, Switzerland
DEATH: July 2, 1778 — Ermenonville, France
COMPOSITIONAL MEDIA: chamber music, opera, songs, books
ITEMS OF INTEREST: probably most famous as a philosopher and author of articles, books on music

Rubinstein, Anton Grigorievich

BIRTH: November 28, 1829 — Vykhvatinetz, Russia
DEATH: November 20, 1894 — Peterhof, Russia
TEACHER(S): his mother, Villoing
COMPOSITIONAL MEDIA: orchestra, chamber music, keyboard, choral, opera, songs
ITEMS OF INTEREST: director — Moscow Conservatory; professional pianist

Ruggles, Carl

BIRTH: March 11, 1876 — Marion, MA
DEATH: October 24, 1971 — Bennington, VT
TEACHER(S): Paine
COMPOSITIONAL MEDIA: orchestra, chamber music, keyboard, choral, songs
ITEMS OF INTEREST: friend of Ives; personally destroyed his early works

S

Saint-Saens, Camille (san sähns')

BIRTH: October 9, 1835 — Paris, France
DEATH: December 16, 1921 — Algiers
TEACHER(S): Halevy
COMPOSITIONAL MEDIA: orchestra, chamber music, ballet,
keyboard, choral, opera, songs, theatrical
ITEMS OF INTEREST: child prodigy; pupils included Messager,
Faure, Gigout; best known works include opera "Sampson et Dalila",
symphonic poem "Danse macabre"

Salieri, Antonio

BIRTH: August 18, 1750 — Verona, Italy
DEATH: May 7, 1825 — Vienna, Austrial
TEACHER(S): Pesetti, Gassmann
COMPOSITIONAL MEDIA: orchestra, chamber music, keyboard,
choral, opera
ITEMS OF INTEREST: students included Beethoven, Schubert, Liszt

Salzedo, Carlos (sahl zā' doh)

BIRTH: April 6, 1885 — Arcachon, France
DEATH: August 17, 1961 — Waterville, ME
TEACHER(S): Beriot, Hasselmans
COMPOSITIONAL MEDIA: orchestra, chamber music, books
ITEMS OF INTEREST: professional harpist; teacher Juilliard School,
Curtis Institute; all compositions featured the harp

Salzman, Eric

BIRTH: September 8, 1933 — New York, NY
TEACHER(S): Luening, Ussachevsky, Beeson, Sessions, Babbitt, Petrassi
COMPOSITIONAL MEDIA: chamber music, opera, electronic, books
ITEMS OF INTEREST: compositions incorporate electronic and theatrical elements

Satie, Erik (sah tē´)

BIRTH: May 17, 1866 — Honfleur, France
DEATH: July 1, 1925 — Paris, France
TEACHER(S): Guilmant, d'Indy, Roussel
COMPOSITIONAL MEDIA: orchestra, ballet, keyboard, choral, theatrical
ITEMS OF INTEREST: associate of Debussy, Ravel, Cocteau; his new approaches to composition influenced many composers

Scarlatti, Alessandro

BIRTH: May 2, 1660 — Palermo, Italy
DEATH: October 24, 1725 — Naples, Italy
TEACHER(S): Carissimi
COMPOSITIONAL MEDIA: chamber music, harpsichord, choral, opera
ITEMS OF INTEREST: choir master — to Queen Christina of Sweden, to Viceroy at Naples, Santa Maria Maggiore in Rome, Cappella reale in Naples; pupils included Hasse, Geminiani, Domenico Scarlatti (his son); best known works include development of opera seria

Scarlatti, Domenico

BIRTH: October 26, 1685 — Naples, Italy
DEATH: July 23, 1757 — Madrid, Spain
TEACHER(S): Alessandro Scarlatti (his father), Gasparini
COMPOSITIONAL MEDIA: harpsichord, choral, opera

ITEMS OF INTEREST: choir master — to Queen of Poland, St. Peter's; teacher — Princess Maria Barbara; best known for keyboard music

Scheidt, Samuel (shīt)

BIRTH: November 3, 1587 — Halle, Germany
DEATH: March 24, 1654 — Halle, Germany
TEACHER(S): Sweelinck
COMPOSITIONAL MEDIA: chamber music, organ, choral
ITEMS OF INTEREST: developed organ style of chorale

Schein, Johann Hermann (shīn)

BIRTH: January 20, 1586 — Grünhain, Saxony
DEATH: November 19, 1630 — Leipzig, Germany
COMPOSITIONAL MEDIA: chamber music, choral
ITEMS OF INTEREST: introduced Italian instrumental style to German music

Schillinger, Joseph

BIRTH: August 31, 1895 — Kharkov, Russia
DEATH: March 23, 1943 — New York, NY
TEACHER(S): Tcherepnin, Wihto
COMPOSITIONAL MEDIA: orchestra, chamber music, keyboard, songs
ITEMS OF INTEREST: settled in New York, 1928; teacher — New School for Social Research, Columbia University Teachers' College, privately with correspondence course; pupils included Gershwin; composition based on mathematical principles

Schnabel, Artur (shnah' bel)

BIRTH: April 17, 1882 — Lipnik, Austria
DEATH: August 15, 1951 — Morschach, Switzerland

TEACHER(S): Leschetizky
COMPOSITIONAL MEDIA: orchestra, chamber music, keyboard, songs
ITEMS OF INTEREST: child prodigy, professional pianist, settled in New York, 1939

Schoenberg, Arnold

BIRTH: September 13, 1874 — Vienna, Austria
DEATH: July 13, 1951 — Los Angeles, CA
TEACHER(S): Zemlinsky
COMPOSITIONAL MEDIA: orchestra, chamber music, keyboard, choral, opera, songs, concert band, books
ITEMS OF INTEREST: teacher — numerous colleges in Germany and U.S.; pupils included Berg, Webern, Wellesz, Kirchner, Kim, Cage; compositions incorporate twelve-tone techniques; best known works include operas "Erwartung", "Moses und Aron", orchestral piece "Verklärte Nacht", composition for a speaker and chamber group "Pierrot lunaire"

Schubert, Franz Peter

BIRTH: January 31, 1797 — Lichtenthal, Austria
DEATH: November 19, 1828 — Vienna, Austria
COMPOSITIONAL MEDIA: orchestra, chamber music, keyboard, choral, opera, songs, theatrical
ITEMS OF INTEREST: although much of his work is highly respected and still performed (i.e. orchestral work "The Unfinished Symphony", chamber peice "The Trout Quintet", Ecossaises for piano), best known works include his songs and song cycles including "Die schone Müllerin", "Erlkönig"

Schuller, Gunther

BIRTH: November 22, 1925 — New York, NY
COMPOSITIONAL MEDIA: orchestra, chamber music, ballet,

keyboard, choral, opera, songs, jazz, concert band, books
ITEMS OF INTEREST: teacher — Manhattan School of Music, Yale
University; president — New England Conservatory, Boston; professional hornist; compositions incorporate serial techniques, jazz
elements; advocate of third stream music combining jazz and classical
elements

Schuman, William

BIRTH: August 4, 1910 — New York, NY
TEACHER(S): Haubiel, Harris
COMPOSITIONAL MEDIA: orchestra, chamber music, keyboard,
choral, opera, songs, concert band
ITEMS OF INTEREST: teacher — Sarah Lawrence College; presi-
dent — Juilliard School, Lincoln Center for the Performing Arts in
New York; Pulitzer Prize winner

Schumann, Clara Josephine

BIRTH: September 13, 1819 — Leipzig, Germany
DEATH: May 20, 1896 — Frankfurt, Germany
TEACHER(S): her father, Wieck
COMPOSITIONAL MEDIA: chamber music, keyboard, songs
ITEMS OF INTEREST: wife of Robert Schumann; best known works
include editing her husband's works

Schumann, Robert

BIRTH: June 8, 1810 — Zwickau, Saxony
DEATH: July 29, 1856 — Endenich, Germany
TEACHER(S): Wieck, Dorn
COMPOSITIONAL MEDIA: orchestra, chamber music, keyboard,
choral, songs, theatrical, books
ITEMS OF INTEREST: professional pianist; teacher — Leipzig
Conservatory; his piano pieces, especially "Album for the Young", is
an important part of today's piano pedagogy; developed mechanical

device to strengthen his right hand which caused an injury that
ended his career

Schütz, Heinrich

BIRTH: October 8, 1585 — Köstritz, Thuringia
DEATH: November 6, 1672 — Dresden
TEACHER(S): G. Gabrieli
COMPOSITIONAL MEDIA: chamber music, choral, opera, songs
ITEMS OF INTEREST: composed first German opera "Dafne"
(manuscript now lost)

Schwartz, Elliot

BIRTH: January 19, 1936 — Brooklyn, NY
TEACHER(S): Beeson, Luening, Creston, Brant, Chou, Wolpe,
Varèse
COMPOSITIONAL MEDIA: orchestra, chamber music, electronic
ITEMS OF INTEREST: teacher — University of Massachusetts,
Bowdoin College

Scriabin, Alexander Nikolaievich (skryah' bin)

BIRTH: January 6, 1872 — Moscow, Russia
DEATH: April 27, 1915 — Moscow, Russia
TEACHER(S): Taneiev, Arensky
COMPOSITIONAL MEDIA: orchestra, keyboard
ITEMS OF INTEREST: teacher — Moscow Conservatory; composi-
tions incorporate whole-tone scales, unique chords, lighting effects

Serebrier, José

BIRTH: December 3, 1938 — Montevideo, Uruguay
TEACHER(S): Giannini, Copland
COMPOSITIONAL MEDIA: orchestra, chamber music, keyboard,
choral, songs
ITEMS OF INTEREST: settled in U.S., 1950

Sessions, Roger

BIRTH: December 28, 1896 — Brooklyn, NY
DEATH: March 16, 1985 — New York, NY
TEACHER(S): Parker, Bloch
COMPOSITIONAL MEDIA: orchestra, chamber music, keyboard, choral, opera, songs, theatrical, books
ITEMS OF INTEREST: teacher — Smith College, Cleveland Institute of Music, Princeton University, University of California/Berkeley, Juilliard School; pupils included Babbitt, Cone, Finney, Imbrie, Kirchner, Kim, Martino; compositions incorporate twelve-tone techniques

Shapey, Ralph

BIRTH: March 12, 1921 — Philadelphia, PA
TEACHER(S): Wolpe
COMPOSITIONAL MEDIA: orchestra, chamber music, keyboard, choral, songs
ITEMS OF INTEREST: teacher — University of Pennsylvania, University of Chicago

Shostakovich, Dmitri Dmitrievich (shôh stáh kōh' vitch)

BIRTH: September 25, 1906 — St. Petersburg, Russia
DEATH: August 9, 1975 — Moscow, Russia
TEACHER(S): Steinberg
COMPOSITIONAL MEDIA: orchestra, chamber music, ballet, keyboard, choral, opera, songs, film
ITEMS OF INTEREST: teacher — Leningrad Conservatory, Moscow Conservatory

Sibelius, Jean (sǐ bā' lyoos)

BIRTH: December 8, 1865 — Tavastehus, Finland
DEATH: September 20, 1957 — Järvenpää
TEACHER(S): Wegelius, R. Fuchs, K. Goldmark

COMPOSITIONAL MEDIA: orchestra, chamber music, keyboard, choral, opera, songs, theatrical

ITEMS OF INTEREST: much of his is nationalistic (based on Finnish themes), stopped composing in 1929, best known works include orchestral piece "Finlandia"

Siegmeister, Elie

BIRTH: January 15, 1909—New York, NY   DEATH: March 10, 1991

TEACHER(S): Riegger, N. Boulanger

COMPOSITIONAL MEDIA: orchestra, chamber music, keyboard, opera, songs, books

ITEMS OF INTEREST: teacher — Hofstra University, collector of folk songs

Slonimsky, Nicolas

BIRTH: April 27, 1894 — St. Petersburg

TEACHER(S): Steinberg

COMPOSITIONAL MEDIA: orchestra, chamber music, keyboard, songs, books

ITEMS OF INTEREST: settled in U.S., 1923; teacher — various institutions

Smetana, Bedrich (smĕh´ tah nah)

BIRTH: March 2, 1824 — Leitomischl, Czechoslovakia

DEATH: May 12, 1884 — Prague, Czechoslovakia

TEACHER(S): Kittl

COMPOSITIONAL MEDIA: orchestra, chamber music, keyboard, choral, opera, songs

ITEMS OF INTEREST: child prodigy; became deaf in 1874; best known works include opera "The Bartered Bride", orchestral theme "The Moldau" (contained in the symphonic poem "Ma Vlast"); died insane

Smith, Hale

BIRTH: June 29, 1925 — Cleveland, OH
COMPOSITIONAL MEDIA: orchestra, chamber music, keyboard, choral, songs, jazz, concert band
ITEMS OF INTEREST: teacher — C.W. Post College, University of Connecticut

Sondheim, Stephen

BIRTH: March 22, 1930 — New York, NY
TEACHER(S): Babbit
COMPOSITIONAL MEDIA: songs, theatrical
ITEMS OF INTEREST: best known works include Broadway shows "Company," "A Little Night Music"

Sousa, John Philip (soo′ ză)

BIRTH: November 6, 1854 — Washington, DC
DEATH: March 6, 1932 — Reading, PA
TEACHER(S): Esputa, Bankert
COMPOSITIONAL MEDIA: opera, concert band, books
ITEMS OF INTEREST: the March King; best known works include "The Stars and Stripes Forever," "El Capitan," "The Washington Post," "Semper Fidelis"

Sowerby, Leo

BIRTH: May 1, 1895 — Grand Rapids, MI
DEATH: July 7, 1968 — Port Clinton, OH
TEACHER(S): Lampert, Andersen
COMPOSITIONAL MEDIA: orchestra, chamber music, keyboard, choral, songs
ITEMS OF INTEREST: teacher — American Conservatory; director — College for Church Musicians, National Cathedral, Washington; Pulitzer Prize winner

Spohr, Ludwig (shpor)

BIRTH: April 5, 1784 — Braunschweig, Germany
DEATH: October 22, 1859 — Kassel, Germany
TEACHER(S): Riemenschneider, Dufour, Hartung, Maucourt
COMPOSITIONAL MEDIA: orchestra, chamber music, keyboard,
choral, opera, songs, books
ITEMS OF INTEREST: professional violinist

Stamitz, Johann Wenzel Anton

BIRTH: June 19, 1717 — Havlickuv Brod, Bohemia
DEATH: March 27, 1757 — Mannheim, Germany
COMPOSITIONAL MEDIA: orchestra, chamber music
ITEMS OF INTEREST: professional violinist; pupils included Karl (his
son), Cannabich

Stamitz, Karl Philipp

BIRTH: May 7, 1745 — Mannheim, Germany
DEATH: November 9, 1801 — Jena, Germany
TEACHER(S): J.W.A. Stamitz (his father), Cannabich, Holzbauer,
F.X. Richter
COMPOSITIONAL MEDIA: orchestra, chamber music, choral,
opera, theatrical
ITEMS OF INTEREST: professional violinist

Starer, Robert

BIRTH: January 8, 1924 — Vienna, Austria
TEACHER(S): Tal, Partos, F. Jacobi
COMPOSITIONAL MEDIA: orchestra, chamber music, ballet,
keyboard, choral, opera, songs
ITEMS OF INTEREST: teacher — Juilliard School, Brooklyn College

Stevens, Halsey

BIRTH: December 3, 1908 — Scott, NY   DEATH: Jan. 20, 1989

TEACHER(S): Bloch
COMPOSITIONAL MEDIA: orchestra, chamber music, keyboard,
songs, books
ITEMS OF INTEREST: teacher — University of Southern California,
authority on the work of Bartók

Still, William Grant

BIRTH: May 11, 1895 — Woodville, MS
DEATH: December 3, 1978 — Los Angeles, CA
TEACHER(S): Varèse, Chadwick
COMPOSITIONAL MEDIA: orchestra, chamber music, ballet,
keyboard, choral, opera, songs, concert band
ITEMS OF INTEREST: compositions incorporate songs of black
America

Stockhausen, Karlheinz

BIRTH: August 22, 1928 — Mödrath, Germany
TEACHER(S): Martin, Messiaen
COMPOSITIONAL MEDIA: orchestra, chamber music, keyboard,
choral, electronic, theatrical
ITEMS OF INTEREST: compositions incorporate serial, aleatoric,
spatial, electronic, graphic techniques

Strang, Gerald

BIRTH: February 13, 1908 — Claresholm, Canada
DEATH: November 2, 1983 — Longbeach, CA
TEACHER(S): Schoenberg, Toch, Koechlin
COMPOSITIONAL MEDIA: orchestra, chamber music, electronic
ITEMS OF INTEREST: worked closely with Schoenberg; teacher at
various S. California colleges; compositions incorporate electronic
techniques

Strauss, Jr., Johann

BIRTH: October 25, 1825 — Vienna, Austria
DEATH: June 3, 1899 — Vienna, Austria
COMPOSITIONAL MEDIA: orchestra, operetta
ITEMS OF INTEREST: best known works include his waltzes in-
cluding "The Blue Danube", "Tales from the Vienna Woods",
operetta "Die Fledermaus"

Strauss, Richard

BIRTH: June 11, 1864 — Munich, Germany
DEATH: September 8, 1949 — Garmisch, Germany
COMPOSITIONAL MEDIA: orchestra, chamber music, ballet,
keyboard, choral, opera, songs
ITEMS OF INTEREST: conductor — various German orchestras;
best known works include operas "Salome", "Der Rosenkavalier",
"Elektra", orchestral works "Don Juan", "Till Eulenspiegel's Merry
Pranks"

Stravinsky, Igor

BIRTH: June 17, 1882 — Oranienbaum, Russia
DEATH: April 6, 1971 — New York, NY
TEACHER(S): Rimsky-Korsakov, V.P. Kalafati
COMPOSITIONAL MEDIA: orchestra, chamber music, ballet,
keyboard, choral, opera, songs, theatrical, jazz, books
ITEMS OF INTEREST: settled in U.S., 1939; compositions incor-
porate a great variety of techniques during development of his career
including extreme dissonance, jazz, bitonality, serial techniques;
although his output was great, best known works include the ballets
"Petrushka", "The Rite of Spring"

Strayhorn, Billy

BIRTH: November 25, 1915 — Dayton, OH
DEATH: May 31, 1967 — New York, NY

COMPOSITIONAL MEDIA: songs, popular, jazz
ITEMS OF INTEREST: co-writer of many of Duke Ellington's greatest works; best known works include "Lush Life," "Take the A Train"

Styne, Jule

BIRTH: December 15, 1905 — London, England
COMPOSITIONAL MEDIA: songs, theatrical, popular
ITEMS OF INTEREST: best known works include Broadway musicals — "Gentlemen Prefer Blondes," "Gypsy," "Funny Girl"

Subotnick, Morton

BIRTH: April 14, 1933 — Los Angeles, CA
TEACHER(S): Milhaud, Kirchner
COMPOSITIONAL MEDIA: chamber music, electronic
ITEMS OF INTEREST: compositions incorporate electronic, mixed media, extra musical sound source, tape techniques, and "ghost" pieces

Sullivan, Arthur Seymour

BIRTH: May 13, 1842 — London, England
DEATH: November 22, 1900 — London, England
TEACHER(S): O'Leary, Haupmann, Goss, Bennett, Helmore
COMPOSITIONAL MEDIA: orchestra, chamber music, ballet, choral, operettas, songs
ITEMS OF INTEREST: collaborated with W.S. Gilbert on some of the most popular operettas of all time including "H.M.S. Pinafore", "The Pirates of Penzance", "The Mikado"

Suppé, Franz von (sōōp' pā)

BIRTH: April 18, 1819 — Spalato, Dalmatia
DEATH: May 21, 1895 — Vienna, Austria
TEACHER(S): Sechter, Seyfried

COMPOSITIONAL MEDIA: orchestra, chamber music, choral, opera and operettas, songs, theatrical
ITEMS OF INTEREST: best known works include "Poet and Peasant" overature from opera of same name

Surinach, Carlos

BIRTH: March 4, 1915 — Barcelona
TEACHER(S): Trapp
COMPOSITIONAL MEDIA: orchestra, chamber music, ballet, keyboard, choral, opera, songs
ITEMS OF INTEREST: settled in New York, 1951; best known works include orchestrated pieces from Albeniz's "Iberia"

T

Tailleferre, Germaine (tī yë fehr')

BIRTH: April 19, 1892—Parc-Saint-Maur, France DEATH: Nov. 7, 1983
TEACHER(S): Ravel
COMPOSITIONAL MEDIA: orchestra, chamber music, ballet, keyboard, choral, opera, songs, theatrical, film, T.V.
ITEMS OF INTEREST:

Tallis, Thomas

BIRTH: 1505
DEATH: November 23, 1585 — Greenwich, England
COMPOSITIONAL MEDIA: keyboard, choral
ITEMS OF INTEREST: organist — Chapel Royal, associate of Byrd

Tartini, Giuseppe

BIRTH: April 8, 1692 — Pirano, Istria
DEATH: February 26, 1770 — Padua, Italy
TEACHER(S): Czernohorsky
COMPOSITIONAL MEDIA: orchestra, chamber music, choral, books
ITEMS OF INTEREST: professional violinist, pupils included Nardini, best known works include violin concertos, sonatas

Taylor, Deems

BIRTH: December 22, 1885 — New York, NY
DEATH: July 3, 1966 — New York, NY
TEACHER(S): Coon
COMPOSITIONAL MEDIA: orchestra, chamber music, keyboard, choral, opera, books
ITEMS OF INTEREST: music critic; radio commentator; president — ASCAP, 1942-48

Tchaikovsky, Piotr Ilich

BIRTH: May 7, 1840 — Votkinsk, Russia
DEATH: November 6, 1893 — St. Petersburg, Russia
TEACHER(S): A. Rubinstein
COMPOSITIONAL MEDIA: orchestra, chamber music, ballet, keyboard, choral, opera, songs
ITEMS OF INTEREST: supported by Nadezhda von Meck; best known works include ballets "Swan Lake" and "Nutcracker", orchestral works "Symphony No. 6 (Pathetique)", "Romeo and Juliet", "Eighteen Twelve Overture", "Capriccio Italien"

Tcherepnin, Alexander Nikolaievich (cheh rep nēn')

BIRTH: January 20, 1899 — St. Petersburg, Russia
DEATH: September 29, 1977 — Paris, France
TEACHER(S): Tiflis, Vidal
COMPOSITIONAL MEDIA: orchestra, chamber music, ballet,

keyboard, choral, opera, songs
ITEMS OF INTEREST: settled in Paris, 1921; moved to U.S.,
1940's; professional pianist; teacher — De Paul University, Chicago;
compositions incorporate folk materials of Russia and the Orient

Telemann, Georg Philipp

BIRTH: March 14, 1681 — Magdeburg, Germany
DEATH: June 25, 1767 — Hamburg, Germany
COMPOSITIONAL MEDIA: orchestra, chamber music, keyboard,
choral, opera
ITEMS OF INTEREST: music director — Sorau, Eisenach, Frankfurt,
Hamburg

Thompson, Randall

BIRTH: April 21, 1899 — New York, NY   DEATH: July 9, 1984
TEACHER(S): Hill, Bloch
COMPOSITIONAL MEDIA: orchestra, chamber music, keyboard,
choral, opera, songs, theatrical
ITEMS OF INTEREST: teacher — Wellesley College, University of
California/Berkeley, Curtis Institute, University of Virginia, Princeton
University, Harvard University

Thomson, Virgil

BIRTH: Nov. 25, 1896—Kansas City, MO   DEATH: Sept. 30, 1989
TEACHER(S): Scalero, N. Boulanger
COMPOSITIONAL MEDIA: orchestra, chamber music, ballet,
keyboard, choral, opera, songs, film
ITEMS OF INTEREST: associate of Gertrude Stein; music critic; best
known works include opera "Four Saints in Three Acts", film score
"The Plough That Broke the Plains"

Toch, Ernst

BIRTH: December 7, 1887 — Vienna, Austria

DEATH: October 1, 1964 — Los Angeles, CA
TEACHER(S): Rehberg
COMPOSITIONAL MEDIA: orchestra, chamber music, keyboard, choral, opera, songs, film
ITEMS OF INTEREST: settled in U.S., 1934; teacher — various institutions including University of California/Los Angeles; Pulitzer Prize winner

Tommasini, Vincenzo

BIRTH: September 17, 1878 — Rome, Italy
DEATH: December 23, 1950 — Rome, Italy
TEACHER(S): Bruch
COMPOSITIONAL MEDIA: orchestra, chamber music, ballet, keyboard, choral, opera, songs, books
ITEMS OF INTEREST: commissioned by Diaghilev to write ballet

Torelli, Giuseppe

BIRTH: April 22, 1658 — Verona, Italy
DEATH: February 8, 1709 — Bologna, Italy
COMPOSITIONAL MEDIA: orchestra, chamber music
ITEMS OF INTEREST: professional violinist

Travis, Roy

BIRTH: June 24, 1922 — New York, NY
TEACHER(S): B. Wagenaar, Luening, Milhaud
COMPOSITIONAL MEDIA: orchestra, chamber music, keyboard, opera, songs
ITEMS OF INTEREST: teacher — Columbia University, Mannes College, University of California/Los Angeles; compositions incorporate electronic techniques, elements of African music

Tudor, David

BIRTH: January 20, 1926 — Philadelphia, PA
TEACHER(S): Wolpe
COMPOSITIONAL MEDIA: chamber music, ballet
ITEMS OF INTEREST: associate of Cage, Feldman; compositions incorporate aleatoric, electronic, visual techniques; composed for Merce Cunningham Dance Company

Turk, Daniel Gottlob

BIRTH: August 10, 1756 — Clausnitz, Saxony
DEATH: August 26, 1813 — Halle, Germany
TEACHER(S): Homilius, J.A. Hiller
COMPOSITIONAL MEDIA: orchestra, keyboard, choral, opera, songs, books
ITEMS OF INTEREST: professional organist, violinist; music director — Halle University

U

Uhlig, Theodor (oo′ lih)

BIRTH: February 15, 1822 — Wurzen, Germany
DEATH: January 3, 1853 — Dresden, Germany
TEACHER(S): F. Schneider
COMPOSITIONAL MEDIA: orchestra, chamber music, keyboard, choral, songs, books
ITEMS OF INTEREST: professional violinist, associate of Wagner, Liszt

Ussachevsky, Vladimir (ōō säh chĕf′ skē)
BIRTH: Nov. 3, 1911 — Hailar, Manchuria   DEATH: Jan 2, 1990
TEACHER(S): Hanson, Bernard Rogers, Luening
COMPOSITIONAL MEDIA: orchestra, chamber music, keyboard, choral, electronic
ITEMS OF INTEREST: teacher — Columbia University, University of Utah; co-director Columbia-Princeton Electronic Music Center; compositions incorporate electronic, tape techniques

V

Van Heusen, James
BIRTH: January 26, 1913 — Syracuse, NY
TEACHER(S): Colburn, Lyman
COMPOSITIONAL MEDIA: songs, popular, film and/or T.V.
ITEMS OF INTEREST: best known works include "Polka Dots and Moonbeams," "Here's That Rainy Day," "Come Fly with Me"

Varèse, Edgard
BIRTH: December 22, 1883 — Paris, France
DEATH: November 6, 1965 — New York, NY
TEACHER(S): d'Indy, Roussel, Widor
COMPOSITIONAL MEDIA: orchestra, chamber music, choral
ITEMS OF INTEREST: settled in New York, 1915; compositions incorporate electronic, extra musical techniques

Vaughan Williams, Ralph

BIRTH: October 12, 1872 — Down Ampney, England
DEATH: August 26, 1958 — London, England
TEACHER(S): C. Wood, W. Parratt, Parry, Stanford, Bruch, Ravel
COMPOSITIONAL MEDIA: orchestra, chamber music, ballet,
keyboard, choral, opera, songs, theatrical, film, concert band, books
ITEMS OF INTEREST: teacher — Royal College of Music, collected
folk songs

Verdi, Giuseppe

BIRTH: October 10, 1813 — Le Roncole, Italy
DEATH: January 27, 1901 — Milan, Italy
TEACHER(S): Vincenzo Lavigna
COMPOSITIONAL MEDIA: chamber music, choral, opera, songs
ITEMS OF INTEREST: best known works include operas "Rigoletto",
"Il Trovatore", "La Traviata", "Aida", "Otello"

Villa-Lobos, Heitor

BIRTH: March 5, 1887 — Rio de Janeiro, Brazil
DEATH: November 17, 1959 — Rio de Janeiro, Brazil
TEACHER(S): his father, Nascimento, Franca, Braga
COMPOSITIONAL MEDIA: orchestra, chamber music, keyboard,
choral, opera, songs
ITEMS OF INTEREST: compositions incorporate Brazilian folk music,
very prolific (over 3,000 works)

Vincent, John

BIRTH: May 17, 1902 — Birmingham, AL
DEATH: January 21, 1977 — Los Angeles, CA
TEACHER(S): Chadwick, Piston, N. Boulanger, Harris
COMPOSITIONAL MEDIA: orchestra, chamber music, ballet, choral,
opera, songs

ITEMS OF INTEREST: teacher — University of California/Los Angeles

Viotti, Giovanni Battista

BIRTH: May 12, 1755 — Fontanetto da Po, Italy
DEATH: March 3, 1824 — London, England
TEACHER(S): Pugnani
COMPOSITIONAL MEDIA: orchestra, chamber music, keyboard
ITEMS OF INTEREST: court musician to Marie Antoinette; director — Italian Opera, Paris; professional violinist

Vivaldi, Antonio

BIRTH: March 4, 1678 — Venice, Italy
DEATH: July 28, 1741 — Vienna, Austria
TEACHER(S): his father, Legrenzi
COMPOSITIONAL MEDIA: orchestra, chamber music, choral, opera, songs
ITEMS OF INTEREST: teacher — Venice, best known works include the concerto grosso "The Seasons"

Vogler, George Joseph (fōg' lĕhr)

BIRTH: June 15, 1749 — Wurzburg, Germany
DEATH: May 6, 1814 — Darmstadt, Germany
TEACHER(S): Padre Martini
COMPOSITIONAL MEDIA: orchestra, chamber music, ballet, keyboard, choral, opera, books
ITEMS OF INTEREST: professional pianist and organist; pupils included Weber, Meyerbeer; published many books on music theory

W

Wagner, Joseph Frederick

BIRTH: January 9, 1900 — Springfield, MA
DEATH: October 12, 1974 — Los Angeles, CA
TEACHER(S): Converse, Casella, N. Boulanger
COMPOSITIONAL MEDIA: orchestra, chamber music, ballet, keyboard, opera, songs, concert band, books
ITEMS OF INTEREST: teacher — Boston University, Brooklyn College, Los Angeles Conservatory, Pepperdine University; author of books on arranging

Wagner, Richard

BIRTH: May 22, 1813 — Leipzig, Germany
DEATH: February 13, 1883 — Venice, Italy
TEACHER(S): Theodor Weinlig
COMPOSITIONAL MEDIA: orchestra, chamber music, keyboard, choral, opera, songs, books
ITEMS OF INTEREST: best known works include operas "Tannhäuser", "Lohengrin", "Der Ring des Nibelungen", "Tristan und Isolde", "Die Meistersinger von Nürnberg"; believed in total balance of music, text and acting; built a theater of his own design in Bayreuth to present his works

Walton, William

BIRTH: March 29, 1902—Oldham, England   DEATH: March 8, 1983
TEACHER(S): his father
COMPOSITIONAL MEDIA: orchestra, chamber music, ballet,
keyboard, choral, opera, songs, film
ITEMS OF INTEREST: best known works include chamber piece
"Facade" for reciter and 6 instruments, oratorio "Belshazzar's Feast"

Ward, Robert

BIRTH: September 13, 1917 — Cleveland, OH
TEACHER(S): Bernard Rogers, Hanson, Jacobi, B. Wagenaar,
Copland
COMPOSITIONAL MEDIA: orchestra, chamber music, keyboard,
choral, opera, songs
ITEMS OF INTEREST: teacher — Columbia University, Juilliard
School; president — North Carolina School of the Arts; active in
music publishing industry; Pulitzer Prize winner

Ward-Steinman, David

BIRTH: November 6, 1936 — Alexandria, LA
TEACHER(S): B. Phillips, N. Boulanger, Riegger, Milhaud, Babbitt
COMPOSITIONAL MEDIA: orchestra, chamber music, ballet,
keyboard, choral, opera, songs, electronic, theatrical, concert band
ITEMS OF INTEREST: teacher — San Diego State College, California State University/San Diego; compositions incorporate electronic,
tape, mixed media techniques

Weber, Carl Maria von

BIRTH: November 18, 1786 — Eutin, Germany
DEATH: June 5, 1826 — London, England
TEACHER(S): M. Haydn, Abbé Vogler
COMPOSITIONAL MEDIA: orchestra, chamber music, keyboard,
choral, opera, songs, theatrical

ITEMS OF INTEREST: best known works include opera "Der Freischütz", "Oberon"

Webern, Anton

BIRTH: December 3, 1883 — Vienna, Austria
DEATH: September 15, 1945 — Mittersill, Germany
TEACHER(S): Guido Adler, Schoenberg
COMPOSITIONAL MEDIA: orchestra, chamber music, keyboard, choral, songs
ITEMS OF INTEREST: compositions incorporate twelve-tone techniques, best known works include "6 Pieces" for orchestra

Weill, Kurt

BIRTH: March 2, 1900 — Dessau, Germany
DEATH: April 3, 1950 — New York, NY
TEACHER(S): Humperdinck, Busoni
COMPOSITIONAL MEDIA: orchestra, chamber music, keyboard, choral, opera, songs, theatrical, film
ITEMS OF INTEREST: settled in U.S., 1935; associate of Bertolt Brecht; compositions incorporate jazz elements; best known for "Threepenny Opera"

Weinberger, Jaromir (vīn' bĕr gĕr)

BIRTH: January 8, 1896 — Prague, Czechoslovakia
DEATH: August 8, 1967 — St. Petersburg, FL
TEACHER(S): Kricka, Karel, Novak, Reger
COMPOSITIONAL MEDIA: orchestra, chamber music, keyboard, choral, opera, songs, concert band
ITEMS OF INTEREST: settled in U.S., 1939

Weiner, Lazar (vī' ner)

BIRTH: Oct. 27, 1897—Cherkassy, Russia   DEATH: Jan. 10, 1982

TEACHER(S): Jacobi, Robert Russell Bennett, Schillinger
COMPOSITIONAL MEDIA: orchestra, chamber music, ballet,
keyboard, choral, opera, songs
ITEMS OF INTEREST: settled in U.S., 1914; teacher — Hebrew
Union College School of Sacred Music; most compositions based on
Jewish subjects

Weingartner, Felix (vĭn′ gart nĕhr)

BIRTH: June 2, 1863 — Zara, Dalmatia
DEATH: May 7, 1942 — Winterthur, Switzerland
TEACHER(S): Reinecke, Jadassohn
COMPOSITIONAL MEDIA: orchestra, chamber music, choral,
opera, songs, books
ITEMS OF INTEREST: conductor of many major opera companies
in Germany; professional pianist

Weisgall, Hugo

BIRTH: October 13, 1912 — Ivančice, Czechoslovakia
TEACHER(S): Sessions, Scalero
COMPOSITIONAL MEDIA: chamber music, ballet, choral, opera,
songs
ITEMS OF INTEREST: settled in U.S., 1920; teacher — Jewish
Theological Seminary in New York, Juilliard School, Queens
College, Peabody Conservatory

Wilder, Alec

BIRTH: Feb. 16, 1907 — Rochester, NY   DEATH: Dec. 22, 1980
COMPOSITIONAL MEDIA: orchestra, chamber music, ballet,
keyboard, opera, songs, theatrical, film, books
ITEMS OF INTEREST: author of book "American Popular Song"

Willan, Healey

BIRTH: October 12, 1880 — Balham, England

DEATH: February 16, 1968 — Toronto, Canada
COMPOSITIONAL MEDIA: orchestra, chamber music, keyboard, choral, opera, songs
ITEMS OF INTEREST: teacher — Royal Conservatory, Toronto and University of Toronto

Wolf, Hugo (volf)

BIRTH: March 13, 1860 — Windisch-Gräz, Austria
DEATH: February 22, 1903 — Vienna, Austria
TEACHER(S): R. Fuchs
COMPOSITIONAL MEDIA: orchestra, chamber music, keyboard, choral, opera, songs
ITEMS OF INTEREST: music critic

Wolpe, Stefan

BIRTH: August 25, 1902 — Berlin, Germany
DEATH: April 4, 1972 — New York, NY
TEACHER(S): Juon, Schreker, Busoni, Webern
COMPOSITIONAL MEDIA: orchestra, chamber music, ballet, keyboard, opera, theatrical
ITEMS OF INTEREST: settled in U.S., 1938; teacher — Settlement Music School in Philadelphia, Philadelphia Academy of Music, Black Mountain College, C.W. Post College, Mannes College; compositions incorporate jazz, Semitic, twelve-tone techniques

Wonder, Stevie

BIRTH: May 13, 1951 — Saginaw, MI
COMPOSITIONAL MEDIA: songs, rock, film and/or T.V.
ITEMS OF INTEREST: a major composer of soul and rock songs; best known works include "You Are the Sunshine of My Life," "Superstition"

Wuorinen, Charles

BIRTH: June 9, 1938 — New York, NY
TEACHER(S): Luening, Beeson, Ussachevsky
COMPOSITIONAL MEDIA: orchestra, chamber music, keyboard, choral, electronic
ITEMS OF INTEREST: teacher — Columbia University, Mannes College of Music; compositions incorporate serial, electronic, tape techniques; Pulitzer Prize winner

X

Xenakis, Yannis

BIRTH: May 29, 1922 — Braila, Rumania
TEACHER(S): Honegger, Milhaud, Messiaen
COMPOSITIONAL MEDIA: orchestra, chamber music, keyboard, books
ITEMS OF INTEREST: teacher — School of Automated Music in Paris, Indiana University; compositions incorporate computer, mathematical techniques

Z

Zador, Eugene

BIRTH: November 5, 1894 — Bátaszék, Hungary
DEATH: April 4, 1977 — Los Angeles, CA
TEACHER(S): Reger

COMPOSITIONAL MEDIA: orchestra, chamber music, ballet, keyboard, choral, opera, songs, film

ITEMS OF INTEREST: teacher — New Vienna Conservatory; settled in U.S., 1939; orchestrator of film scores

Zappa, Frank

BIRTH: Dec. 21, 1940 — Baltimore, MD DEATH: Dec. 4, 1993

COMPOSITIONAL MEDIA: songs, popular, film and/or T.V.

ITEMS OF INTEREST: founder of the musical group Mothers of Invention; combined classical and jazz elements in an innovative rock style

Zimmermann, Bernd Alois

BIRTH: March 20, 1918 — Bliesheim, Germany

DEATH: August 10, 1970 — Königsdorf, Germany

TEACHER(S): Jarnach, Fortner, Leibowitz

COMPOSITIONAL MEDIA: orchestra, chamber music, ballet, keyboard, choral, opera, songs, theatrical, film

ITEMS OF INTEREST: teacher — University of Cologne; compositions incorporate serial, electronic, graphic, mixed media techniques

Zingarelli, Nicola Antonio (tsin gah rel' lē)

BIRTH: April 4, 1752 — Naples, Italy

DEATH: May 5, 1837 — Torre del Greco, Italy

COMPOSITIONAL MEDIA: chamber music, organ, choral, opera, songs

ITEMS OF INTEREST: pupils included Bellini, Mercadante

Theory

NOTES

The symbols used to write music.

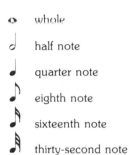

𝗈	whole
𝅗𝅥	half note
𝅘𝅥	quarter note
𝅘𝅥𝅮	eighth note
𝅘𝅥𝅯	sixteenth note
𝅘𝅥𝅰	thirty-second note

NOTE RELATIONSHIPS

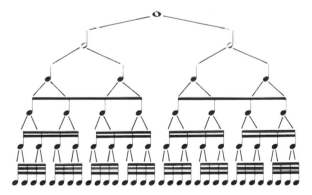

RESTS

The symbols that indicate silence.

▬	whole rest
▬	half rest
𝄽	quarter rest
𝄾	eighth rest
𝄿	sixteenth rest
𝅀	thirty-second rest

REST RELATIONSHIPS

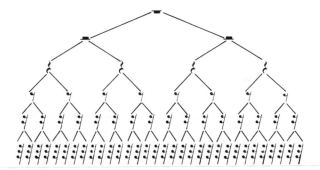

DYNAMIC MARKS

Indications of various degrees of volume.

pp = pianissimo, very soft

p = piano, soft

mp = mezzo piano, moderately soft

mf = mezzo forte, moderately loud

f = forte, loud

ff = fortissimo, very loud

= crescendo, gradually get louder

= diminuendo, gradually get softer

TEMPO MARKS

Tempo markings tell how slow or fast to play the music.

Accelerando.   Gradually get faster.

Adagio.   Slow, between lento and andantino.

Allegretto.   Fast, a little slower than allegro.

Allegro.   Fast.

Andante.   Moderate, walking speed.

Andantino.   A little slower than andante.

Larghetto.   Somewhat faster than largo.

Largo.   Very slow.

Lento.   Slow.

Moderato.   Moderate.

Prestissimo.   As fast as possible.

Presto.   Very fast.

Ritardando.   Gradually get slower.

MUSICAL SYMBOLS

Musical symbols guide the performer in interpreting the composer's wishes.

$\frown$ = Fermata, hold the note longer than its normal value.

$>$ = Accent, play the note a little louder.

$\cdot$ = Staccato, play the note short.

$-$ = Tenuto, hold the note for its full value.

$,$ = Breath mark.

$\%$ = Repeat the previous measure.

$\overset{2}{\%}$ = Repeat the previous two measures.

$\sqcap$ = Down bow.

$\vee$ = Up bow.

SCALE TYPES

Major Scale

Pure Minor (Natural Minor)

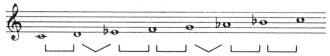

Harmonic Minor

Melodic Minor (Natural Minor Descending)

Chromatic

Whole Tone

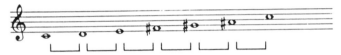

Pentatonic

$\vee$ = half step

$\sqcup$ = whole step

$\undersf{\vee}$ = 1½ steps

KEY SIGNATURES

CIRCLE OF FIFTHS
Major Sharp Keys

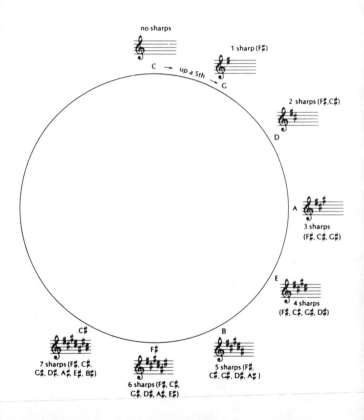

CIRCLE OF FIFTHS
Major Flat Keys

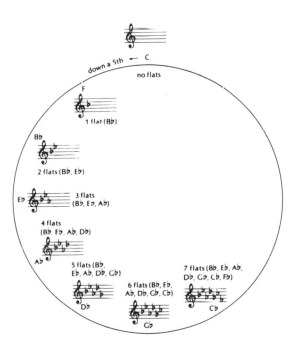

CIRCLE OF FIFTHS
All Major Keys

If we put the sharp keys and the flat keys together, the circle would look like this:

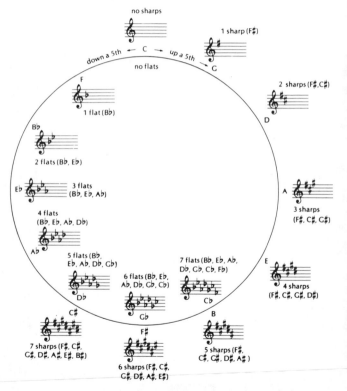

CHORD TYPES

Major

Minor

Diminished

Augmented

Dominant Seventh

Major Seventh

CHORD CHART

x = double sharp   **bb** = double flat

MAJOR SCALES

NATURAL MINOR SCALES

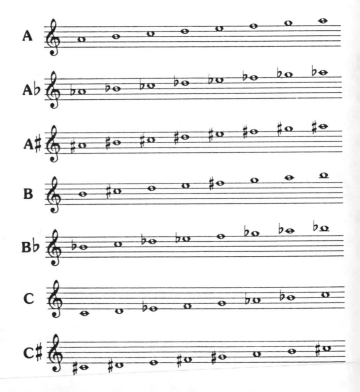

HARMONIC MINOR SCALES

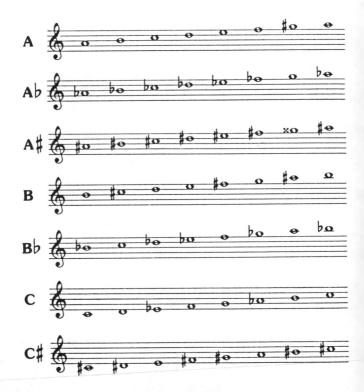

MELODIC MINOR SCALES

(Uses Natural Minor descending)

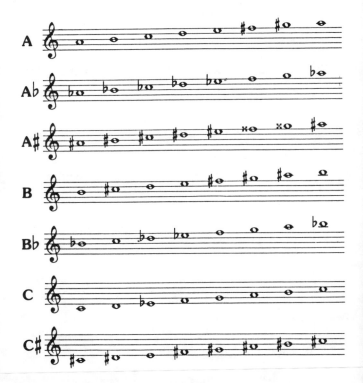

CHART OF VOICE RANGES
FROM LOWEST TO HIGHEST

Bass

Baritone

Tenor

Alto (Contralto)

Soprano